By the Seat
of Their Pants

The Story of Early Aviation

Books by Phil Ault

By the Seat of Their Pants

Their Pants

The Story of Early Aviation

Phil Ault

ILLUSTRATED WITH PHOTOGRAPHS AND MAPS

DODD, MEAD & COMPANY

New York

Illustrations courtesy of: American Airlines, 100; American Hall of Aviation History, 10, 14, 41, 58, 59, 60 *top*, 61, 62, 63, 64, 65 *right*, 71, 80 *bottom*, 116, 168; Ault Photo Studio, 69; Aviation Hall of Fame, Milton Caniff, 22, 28 *top*, 30 *top*, 33, 34, 40, 46, 48, 85, 95, 119 *top*, 133, 137, 163; Lawrence D. Bell Collection, 36–37, 38, 43, 45, 51, 65 *left*, 75, 80 *top*, 104, 106, 111, 112, 146, 151, 206 *top*, 207; British Aircraft Corporation, 208; *Flint Journal*, 170, 173; The Henry Ford Museum, Dearborn, Michigan, 29; General Dynamics Convair Division, 53, 66; *The Honolulu Advertiser*, 175, 178, 181 *top*; Honolulu *Star Bulletin*, 171, 179, 181 *bottom*; *Illustrated World*, 68, 70, 72; Library of Congress, 27, 30 *bottom*, 49, 50, 76, 77, 89, 114, 123; Lockheed Aircraft Corporation, 195, 196, 198, 199, 201, 203; Nassau County Historical Museum, 126, 130, 131, 157; National Air and Space Museum, Smithsonian Institution, 82, 128, 129, 135, 159, 164, 187, 189; Northern Indiana Historical Society, 35; Pan American World Airways, 165; G. P. Putnam's Sons, 17, 19 *bottom*; Ryan Aeronautical Library, 142, 152, 184–185; Santa Ana *Register*, 192; *South Bend Tribune*, 32, 96, 101, 140; Lloyd S. Taylor, 54, 55, 56, 57, 60 *bottom*; United Airlines, 93, 97, 99, 147; U.S. Shipping Board, 19 *top*.

Maps on pages 13 and 202 by Salem Tamer.

1   2   3   4   5   6   7   8   9   10

Library of Congress Cataloging in Publication Data

Ault, Phillip H
By the seat of their pants.

Bibliography: p.
Includes index.
SUMMARY: A history of early aviation with detailed
stories of flights, people, and planes.
1.   Aeronautics—History—Juvenile literature.
[1.   Aeronautics—History]   I.   Title.
TL547.A84   629.13′09   78-7738
ISBN 0-396-07613-0

For Bill, who has flown United States Marine Corps jets at speeds the people in this book never dreamed possible

Contents

*An informal snapshot of Amelia Earhart taken in 1928 as she prepared
for her transatlantic flight*

— 1 —

Out of the Clouds

Dreary masses of cloud hung over the liner S.S. *America* as her prow cut a path of foam through the rolling greenish waters of the Atlantic Ocean off the coast of southern Ireland. Although it was mid-June, those among her hundreds of passengers who walked the decks for after-breakfast exercise had bundled up in coats and sweaters against the moist morning chill. The *America* was two days at sea out of Bremen, Germany, headed for New York City five days away.

A passenger at the rail pointed into the air and exclaimed to his companion, "Look! An airplane. Coming out of the clouds!"

Word of the amazing sight flashed around the ship, causing passengers and crew to cluster on deck. It was startling, truly. This was the year 1928, and only a few pioneer aviators had yet dared to risk their lives by flying their planes over the vast watery stretches of the Atlantic.

As the unexpected plane dove down to a level a few hundred feet above the water and began to circle the *America*, those aboard the ship were able to identify it. The craft was a three-motored seaplane with pontoons in place of wheels, its single wing painted gold and its plywood fuselage bright orange. It was American, that they could tell by the flag painted on its side along with the name, *Friendship*. Obviously those on the plane wanted to communicate with the ship, but how?

In the radio shack of the *America*, the ship's operator sent out

11

the word, "Plane . . . plane," trying to reach the aircraft's operator. He received no reply.

The ship's passengers saw a paper bag, aimed at the *America's* deck, fall like a tiny bomb from an open hatch in the bottom of the circling plane. It missed by two hundred yards, dropping into the sea. Again the plane circled low around the liner's stacks and another weighted bag descended. That missed, too.

Then, as though despairing, the pilot gunned his motors and the airplane vanished into the clouds to the northeast.

"Crazy people!" some of the passengers mumbled.

Passengers aboard the *America* had no way of knowing that the two lost bags, each weighted with an orange, carried a message scribbled by Amelia Earhart: "Which way is Ireland?"

The plight of Miss Earhart and her two men companions in the plane at that moment was critical. They didn't know where they were. The airplane's radio was broken. They had been flying, almost constantly through clouds, rain, and fog, from the American side of the Atlantic since the previous day. The gasoline gauge showed only an hour's fuel remaining. Amelia was a passenger aboard the *Friendship* because she was attempting to become the first woman to fly the Atlantic Ocean. At that moment, the possibility grew ominous that the adventure might end in tragedy rather than triumph, as had three other flights in which women perished while seeking to achieve this goal.

In our day of sleek giant supersonic jets whose courses are set by computer and whose safety is protected by the far-seeing "eyes" of radar, we cannot easily comprehend the enormous risks the first transatlantic flyers took or the flimsy condition of the planes in which they flew. They gambled their lives on a few gallons of gasoline, primitive instruments that frequently failed in flight, and hope for a favorable wind. Yet there were many ready to try. The thrill of fame and success beckoned. They went without life preservers, life rafts, or parachutes in order to cut down the weight of their planes, pitting their skill and luck against the perils of the air. Flying one hundred miles an hour at low levels, they found the width of the Atlantic almost interminable.

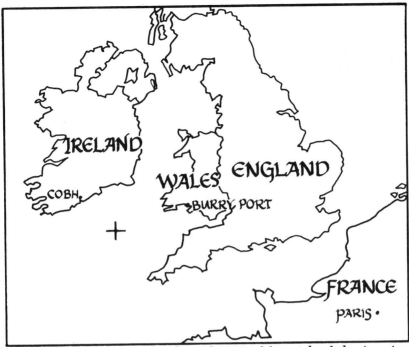

Cross shows approximately where the Friendship *sighted the* America.

Although unknown previously, Amelia Earhart suddenly became the center of world attention while the flight was in progress and the *Friendship*, without a radio, had lost all contact with the earth. Unmarried and twenty-nine years old, the slim woman with short tousled hair and a cool manner was a social worker at Denison House in Boston. She had learned to fly while living in California, and after moving to Boston had joined a flying club. People said she looked like a feminine version of Charles A. Lindbergh, who had thrilled the world a year earlier by flying alone from New York to Paris. She did, indeed.

Flying the Atlantic wasn't Amelia's idea. She was quite happy working with underprivileged Syrian and Chinese children at the settlement house. One day, however, she had a telephone call from a man who asked if she would be interested in making a flight that might be hazardous. Later, she said she had thought the caller might be representing bootleggers who wanted her to fly a

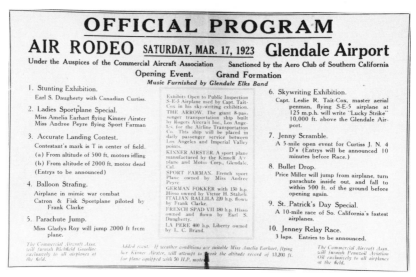

OFFICIAL PROGRAM

AIR RODEO SATURDAY, MAR. 17, 1923 Glendale Airport

Under the Auspices of the Commercial Aircraft Association   Sanctioned by the Aero Club of Southern California

Opening Event.   Grand Formation

Music Furnished by Glendale Elks Band

1. Stunting Exhibition.
   Earl S. Daugherty with Canadian Curtiss.

2. Ladies Sportplane Special.
   Miss Amelia Earhart flying Kinner Airster
   Miss Andree Peyre flying Sport Farman

3. Accurate Landing Contest.
   Contestant's mark is T in center of field.
   (a) From altitude of 500 ft, motors idling
   (b) From altitude of 2000 ft, motor dead
   (Entrys to be announced)

4. Balloon Strafing.
   Airplane in mimic war combat
   Catron & Fisk Sportplane piloted by
   Frank Clarke

5. Parachute Jump.
   Miss Gladys Roy will jump 2000 ft from
   plane.

Exhibits Open to Public Inspection
S-E-5 Airplane used by Capt. Tait-
Cox in his sky-writing exhibition.
THE ARROW. The giant 8-pas-
senger transportation ship built
by Rogers Aircraft Inc., Los Ange-
les, for the Airline Transportation
Co. This ship will be placed in
daily passenger service between
Los Angeles and Imperial Valley
points.
KINNER AIRSTER. A sport plane
manufactured by the Kinner Air-
plane and Motor Corp, Glendale,
Cal.
SPORT FARMAN. French sport
Plane owned by Miss Andree
Peyre
GERMAN FOKKER with 150 h.p.
Hisso owned by Victor H. Staheli
ITALIAN BALLILA 220 h.p. flown
by Frank Clarke.
FRENCH SPAD VII 180 h.p. Hisso
owned and flown by Earl S.
Daugherty.
LA PERE 400 h.p. Liberty owned
by L. C. Brand.

6. Skywriting Exhibition.
   Capt. Leslie R. Tait-Cox, master aerial
   penman, flying S-E-5 airplane at
   125 m.p.h. will write "Lucky Strike"
   10,000 ft. above the Glendale Airport.

7. Jenny Scramble.
   A 5-mile open event for Curtiss J. N. 4
   D's (Entrys will be announced 10
   minutes before Race.)

8. Bullet Drop.
   Price Miller will jump from airplane, turn
   parachute inside out, and fall to
   within 500 ft. of the ground before
   opening again.

9. St. Patrick's Day Special.
   A 10-mile race of So. California's fastest
   airplanes.

10. Jenney Relay Race.
    3 laps. Entries to be announced.

The Commercial Aircraft Assn. will furnish Richfield Gasoline exclusively to all airplanes at the field.

Added event. If weather conditions are suitable Miss Amelia Earhart, flying her Kinner Airster, will attempt to break the altitude record of 13,200 ft. for plane equipped with 30 H.P. motor.

The Commercial Aircraft Assn. will furnish Pennzoil Aviation Oil exclusively to all airplanes at the field.

This 1923 program shows the kinds of stunts that thrilled air show crowds in the early 1920's. One of the entrants in Event No. 2 was Amelia Earhart, then a novice pilot flying the first airplane she owned. Five years later, she flew the Atlantic.

load of liquor illegally into the United States. This was during Prohibition, when the manufacture and sale of alcoholic beverages was forbidden.

Satisfied that the call was legitimate, she agreed to meet the man. When she did he asked, "Should you like to fly the Atlantic?"

After hearing the rest of the story, she quickly said yes. Mrs. Frederick Guest of London, a wealthy, transplanted American woman from Pittsburgh, was a strong advocate of woman's equality and was anxious to show that women, too, had the bravery to fly the ocean. She purchased a Fokker plane, originally intending to make the flight herself as a passenger with two men doing the actual flying. She hired Wilmer Stultz, an expert military and commercial pilot, to fly the plane and Lou Gordon, another experienced airman, to be the flight mechanic and relief pilot.

Then Mrs. Guest decided not to risk the flight herself. Her agents were instructed to find a young woman who knew how to fly and was willing to make the trip. Their search led them to Amelia Earhart.

Preparations were made in secret at Boston harbor. A direct nonstop flight from Boston to Great Britain was impossible, because the *Friendship* wouldn't be able to get off the water carrying enough gasoline for that trip. So, without fanfare, the *Friendship* flew to Trepassey, Newfoundland, stopping overnight at Halifax, Nova Scotia. The plan was to fly the Atlantic from Trepassey to Ireland, more than two thousand miles over the water, taking off from the bay near the fishing village.

News of the attempt spread across the United States while Amelia, Stultz, and Gordon waited at Trepassey for suitable weather conditions. In those days, information about the frequently turbulent weather over the Atlantic was skimpy and often inaccurate. A few ships at sea radioed weather condition reports to New York; by the time they were compared and the information sent by telephone to Trepassey, it was many hours out of date.

The flyers had intended to stay in Trepassey only two days for refueling and final preparations. Weather conditions turned so bad, however, that the restless, anxious trio had to wait thirteen days. This seemed almost like years to them. Back in the United States, interest dwindled in their flight because nothing was happening.

Finally, on Sunday morning, the seventeenth of June, the weather at Trepassey and over the Atlantic seemed good enough to attempt a takeoff.

The flyers knew that at best the takeoff would be perilous. If they succeeded in getting into the air, it would be by the narrowest of margins. Unlike most long-distance flight attempts in the hectic, air-crazy days of the late 1920's, this was being done in a seaplane. Instead of one engine it had three, one in the nose and the other two suspended from the fuselage under each wing. The *Friendship* had been built by the Fokker company with wheels, but for this trip these had been replaced by pontoons, suspended from the fuselage by thin metal rods. The plane had to land on and take off from water. This made it possible in theory for Amelia and her companions to come down on the surface of the ocean safely in an emergency. Landing in rough ocean waters, however, the *Friendship* was likely to capsize or break apart before help could reach it.

Three motors instead of one appeared to add safety, too. But three motors drank far more of the precious gasoline supply than a single one, which meant that every possible drop must be carried. Each motor, incidentally, developed 225 horsepower, about what a compact automobile does today. All together, they had to lift six tons of plane and load from the dragging water.

Stultz taxied the *Friendship* out into the bay. Amelia and Gordon crouched in the rear of the fuselage, to balance the load. She held a stopwatch to check on the takeoff speed. Stultz gave the plane the gun and it bounced forward slowly, then a little faster. Water from the waves splashed against the engines, making them sputter. Forty miles an hour. Forty-five. But not enough. The plane had to be going at least fifty miles an hour before it could rise.

Back to the fishing village they went. Amelia and Gordon unloaded several five-gallon cans of gasoline which were carried loose as an extra reserve. Once more the *Friendship* strained to become airborne but failed. Back to the dock again. This time they put ashore the remaining cans of extra gasoline and everything else they could spare, keeping only a single duffle bag of personal items, a thermos jug of coffee, and a lunch box of sandwiches, cookies, oranges, malted milk tablets, chocolate bars, and an emergency ration of pemmican. The *Friendship* was stripped down to the bone; it carried almost nothing except the three aviators and seven hundred gallons of gasoline.

On the third try the lightened plane crept up to sixty miles an hour. Stultz pulled back the stick, and to the delight of her crew the *Friendship* rose a few feet above the water. Next stop, the British Isles! Perhaps.

Grudgingly the *Friendship* rose to three thousand feet, even more reluctantly to five thousand. Stultz exchanged radio messages with a ship off Cape Race, Newfoundland. Then the first sign of trouble developed. The plane nosed into a snowstorm and after that into clouds so thick the flyers no longer could see the ocean, and most of the time not the sky, either.

16

Photograph of the Friendship *taking off is from Amelia Earhart's book,* Twenty Hours, Forty Minutes, *published in 1929 by G. P. Putnam's Sons.*

They droned along at about a hundred miles an hour until evening. Stultz was at the controls most of the time, with relief from Gordon. The plan for Amelia to do her share of the piloting had to be abandoned because she had no training in instrument flying. Crude as the instruments were, they were the only means by which the adventurers could tell which way they were going.

The wooden-walled cabin of the Fokker had been intended to carry passengers over land. All seats had been removed and two auxiliary gasoline tanks installed. A narrow passage between the tanks led from the cockpit to the rear of the cabin. Amelia spent most of her time standing in this passageway, so she could feel a little of the heat from the cabin, lying down, or kneeling at a small table used for navigation calculations.

As best she could, she scrawled notes into a logbook. After night fell, she wrote in the dark, using her thumb as the guide for each line.

During one glimpse of the water below, she wrote, "The sea looks like the back of an elephant, the same kind of wrinkles."

17

An ominous note crept into the log several hours into the flight: "Bill says radio is cuckoo."

The long northern twilight turned into darkness, and Stultz discovered that he could not read the radium figures on the compass. The instrument panel was without electric light. Gordon solved the problem by rigging a flashlight so that its beam struck the compass dial. Stultz tried to get the plane above the clouds by rising to five thousand feet, then, hating to burn up the gasoline necessary to do so, to ten thousand feet, but still they were encased in fog.

Early the next morning found the *Friendship* still fogbound, plunging ahead through a blind gray world. Stultz took the plane to a lower altitude. The situation was becoming increasingly uneasy.

Amelia wrote in the log, "Instrument flying. Slow descent, first. Going down fast. It takes a lot to make my ears hurt. 5000 now. Awfully wet. Water dripping in window. Port motor coughing. Sounds as if all motors are cutting. Bill opens her wide to try to clear. Sounds rotten on the right."

The plane continued to nose down through the overcast as dawn cast a pink shadow on the fog.

Another entry in the log: "Himmel! The sea! Patchy clouds. We have been jazzing from 1000 to 5000 where we are now, to get out of the clouds . . . the sea for awhile . . . port motor off again . . . can't use radio at all. Coming down in a rather clear spot. Everything sliding forward."

By now, the flyers believed, they should be near Ireland if they were on course. But were they? No way existed for them to check.

At 8:50 A.M., Amelia scribbled a jubilant note in the log: "2 boats!!!!"

It was encouraging to have evidence that there were other human beings in existence. But the trio had no way to communicate with the two small fishing boats. Then came an even more welcome sight, a large transatlantic steamship.

"Try to get bearing," Amelia wrote in her staccato notes. "Radio won't. One hour's gas. Mess. All craft cutting our course. Why?"

The flyers were puzzled and worried. If they were on the cor-

What passengers on the America saw. A photographer on the deck of the America took this picture of the Friendship *as it "bombed" the liner with messages dropped in paper bags weighted with oranges.*

What the flyers on the Friendship *saw. Amelia took this picture of the* America *through the open hatch in the bottom of the* Friendship's *fuselage.*

rect east-west course, the ship should be sailing west toward the United States along a route parallel to theirs. Instead, it was cutting at an angle across their path. Surely, the ship with its instruments and navigators wouldn't be wrong. How had the plane drifted off course? Which way was it to the British Isles, and were the flyers really headed that way? With only an hour's gasoline supply remaining, they didn't have a drop to spare for maneuvering around.

They felt frustrated, circling a few hundred feet above the huge liner, anxious to learn from it what their position was but unable to reach those aboard it. That was when Amelia dropped the two messages, weighted with uneaten oranges from the lunch box. The flyers hoped that after receiving one of them, the *America*'s captain would have sailors chalk a huge arrow and the ship's navigational position on the deck. Actually, Captain George H. Fried had ordered crewmen to do precisely that, but since he hadn't expected to see the *Friendship* they couldn't get the task done in time. The vessel was seventy-two miles southeast of Cobh, Ireland.

The flyers didn't have enough gasoline to continue circling the *America*. They talked quickly among themselves above the roar of the motors. Should they land the plane alongside the *America* and give up their flight? They knew they would be unable to take off again in the rough seas. Or should they press ahead on the course they had been flying for the hour of flight the gasoline supply left them, despite the baffling conflict in courses? If they did the latter, they might be forced to land in the sea with gasoline tanks empty and no ship nearby to rescue them.

With no life-saving equipment aboard, it was an all-or-nothing gamble.

All nodded their heads in agreement. "Let's go ahead."

Unaware of the full extent of the drama going on above them, the passengers of the *America* saw the plane pull away from the ship and resume its course. Stultz held the *Friendship* barely five hundred feet above the ocean, just under the low cloud ceiling. Half an hour later, the three flyers sighted a few fishing vessels. Then, land! The gauge showed only a few gallons of gasoline left in the tanks. With it, Stultz brought the *Friendship* down into a bay outside a town. He taxied it to a buoy floating offshore. They were safe, but where were they?

A few people on shore looked at them, then went about their own business. Gordon called out the window for a boat to bring them ashore. No reply.

"I'll get their attention," Amelia said. She waved a towel out the window. A man ashore took off his coat and waved back but made no other effort to reach them. Nearly an hour passed before the first boats came out from shore to see who the aerial visitors were and what they wanted.

Only then did the *Friendship*'s crew learn that they had landed at Burry Port, Wales. Amelia Earhart had indeed become the first woman to fly the Atlantic Ocean. They learned, too, the reason why the *America* had been sailing across their path at such an angle. The flyers had thought they were approaching Ireland, but they already had passed that island and were flying across the open water between southeastern Ireland and Wales. The *America* had been emerging from the broad channel between the two countries and had not yet set its westward course for New York.

The world was jubilant at the news of the *Friendship*'s successful landing. For hours the plane had been so completely out of touch that many persons believed it had fallen into the ocean, as numerous other would-be transatlantic planes had done. When the three crew members flew on to Southampton, England, and then visited London, tremendous enthusiasm welcomed them.

Even though Amelia Earhart hadn't piloted the plane a single mile of its long journey, she was the center of attention. This embarrassed her, because she knew that most of the glory belonged to Wilmer Stultz, the pilot. She said so, but hardly anyone listened. She quickly became a world heroine. If Stultz didn't receive the praise he deserved, he did have the consolation of being paid $20,000, a very large sum in those days, by Mrs. Guest for his work. Lou Gordon received $5,000. Amelia didn't receive a penny, nor had she expected to be paid. Her reward came in her satisfaction of being the first woman to fly the ocean and proving that women could be as audacious as men.

Amelia Earhart

That flight happened when airplanes were just becoming large and strong enough for aviators to risk flying them over wide stretches of water. When anyone wanted to travel between America and Europe then, the only way to go was by ship.

Scores of passenger ships were at sea every day on the steamship track between North America and Europe. On a typical day in June, 1928, the month of the *Friendship*'s flight, seven liners sailed from New York for such British and European ports as Southampton; LeHavre, France; and Bremen, Germany; and as many departed westbound from Europe. Big liners like the *America* and the *Leviathan* carried a thousand passengers or more, and had crews of five hundred men and women to sail the ship and serve the guests.

Shipboard life was a private world all its own. Deck games such as shuffleboard and horse racing with small wooden horses whose movements were determined by shakes of dice entertained the passengers. Each noon a lottery was held in which passengers guessed how many miles their ship had traveled during the past twenty-four hours, usually 250 to 500 miles. On the final night before reaching port, a captain's dinner with paper streamers, balloons, and funny hats like a New Year's Eve party was the climax of the voyage. Well-to-do passengers on the upper decks traveled first class in spacious cabins, while deep down in the ship near the waterline third-class passengers traveling cheaply occupied small cabins, many of them without windows. Some vessels even had steerage areas, where immigrants going to a new life in America huddled together with almost no facilities.

Nobody aboard the *America* that day, or the three aviators in the *Friendship*, would have guessed that jet-powered airplanes would one day almost wipe transatlantic travel by ship out of existence. Instead of being at sea five days to a week, travelers can cross from New York to London in only a few hours. They fly at an altitude of thirty thousand feet or more above the fog and clouds that endangered the *Friendship*, and often aren't even aware that they are over the ocean. A transatlantic flight today is entirely unlike the one Amelia Earhart and her companions endured on their pioneering venture. The passengers find it far smoother riding than the rolling and tossing of a ship. Four million persons fly between the United States and Great Britain each year.

Down on the ocean itself, only an occasional passenger liner makes the crossing. Usually its passengers are persons with time and money, looking for novelty, people whose friends sometimes say, "They must be crazy, going by ship."

Amelia's successful flight in 1928 demonstrated how far aviation had advanced since man's first heavier-than-air flight was made by the Wright brothers in 1903. Marvelous as it seemed at the time, the *Friendship*'s flight was barely the beginning of the modern air age we have come to know. What we have today could not exist had it not been for those daring men and women in ill-equipped, rickety aircraft who flew into adventure by the seat of their pants.

— 2 —

Sticks and Canvas

The wonder of it is that the first airplanes flew at all. They were merely collections of sticks, canvas, and piano wire that looked more like box kites than the aircraft we know. Their feeble power was supplied by tiny gasoline engines. They were piloted by foolhardy men who believed that they had solved the mystery of flight, which had intrigued humans for thousands of years.

From ancient times, men wondered why birds could fly but they could not. What magic trick did these little creatures know, so they could soar into the sky while men, far more intelligent, could not get off the ground?

This challenge of flight baffled humans and frustrated them. The Greeks had a myth about Icarus, who used the wings his father, Daedalus, had made and flew too close to the sun. Its heat melted the wax on the wings and he plunged to his death in the sea. Down through the centuries, wise men studied the birds and attempted to imitate them with flapping wings. The renowned artist-scientist Leonardo da Vinci in the 1400's drew sketches of a machine to fly, but to no avail. While humans have occupied the earth for many thousands of years, no person ever was able to rise off its surface until less than two hundred years ago.

Two Frenchmen became the first humans to look down on the earth from aloft when they rose into the air aboard a hot air balloon in Paris in November, 1783. This balloon, built by the Montgolfier brothers, floated free into the atmosphere when a fire of straw and wood heated the air in its silken bag. The balloonists continued to stoke the airborne fire in their gondola as they rose to three thousand feet over the astonished people of the French capital. They drifted ten miles in twenty-three minutes and landed safely.

A balloon ascension was marvelous to the men and women of the 1780's. The earth had a new dimension for them. This wasn't flying, however. That could be done only if the aerial craft was powered by a motor of some kind and could be controlled to go wherever its pilot desired. Steam engines were too heavy. Around 1900, after experimenting with gliders, inventors began trying to put small internal combustion gasoline engines, developed for the new-fangled automobiles that were just appearing on the road, into craft resembling gliders.

The most famous American in this work of trying to invent the airplane was the eminent secretary of the Smithsonian Institution, Samuel P. Langley. With considerable fanfare, he assembled a craft he called an Aerodrome, from the Greek word meaning "air runner." This Aerodrome was placed atop a houseboat in the Potomac River near Washington in October, 1903, at the end of a seventy-foot track. Langley's assistant, Charles Manly, was at the controls. Newspapermen and spectators gathered to watch what Langley was positive would be man's first heavier-than-air powered flight. Its fifty horsepower engine *putt-putt*ing, the Aerodrome rolled down the track to the end of the houseboat— and fell kerplunk into the river. "Like a handful of mortar," one reporter wrote. Fortunately, Manly was rescued from the submerged wreckage.

Ridicule greeted the failure. *The New York Times* observed sarcastically in an editorial, "The flying machine which will really fly might be evolved by the combined and continuous efforts of mathematicians and mechanicians in from one to ten million years."

Despite this fiasco, Langley and Manly tried again. The Aerodrome was hauled from the Potomac, repaired, and given another try two months later, on December 8. Again it flopped off the end

Men were first lifted into the air when balloon ascensions were made in Paris in the 1780's. The balloons were filled with hot air.

Samuel P. Langley

Langley's Aerodrome *hopefully illustrated in flight.*

In this comfortable home at Dayton, Ohio, the Wright brothers, Wilbur and Orville, grew up. Along with their bicycle shop, the family home has been moved to Henry Ford's Greenfield Village in Dearborn, Michigan.

of the houseboat into the river and sank. Men apparently just weren't meant to fly.

While the nation snorted at Langley's attempts, two unknown brothers who ran a bicycle shop in Dayton, Ohio, Orville and Wilbur Wright, had set up a camp on the sandy, windswept Outer Banks of North Carolina near the tiny community of Kitty Hawk. The Atlantic Ocean shore was a few hundred yards away. Except for the men at a Life Saving Station nearby, hardly anyone knew about the young Ohioans and the flimsy machine they kept in a shed next to the shack in which they were living. Quiet men, the two avoided publicity.

Orville and Wilbur had been at Kitty Hawk before, testing their ideas about the mysterious science of aerodynamics with gliders launched from Kill Devil Hill, a high point above the sandy plain. By mid-December, 1903, they were ready to test the glider-like craft in which they had installed a weak thirteen-horsepower gasoline engine built for them by Charles Taylor, their bicycle-shop assistant. The engine was mounted beside the

29

Charles Taylor

Man's first powered flight is caught by the camera as the Wright brothers' plane leaves the ground at Kitty Hawk, North Carolina, with Orville at the controls and Wilbur running alongside.

pilot, who lay face down on the lower of the two wings, entirely unprotected. Chains similar to those on a bicycle were driven by this motor and turned two wooden propellors. These pushed the plane forward, rather than pulling it as modern engines do. Instead of using flapping wings like those of birds, the Wrights used stiff, fixed wings supplemented by movable panels to steer the plane.

By a flip of the coin, Orville placed himself at the controls of the *Flyer*, as they called the craft, on the morning of December 17, 1903. The wind was blowing across the dunes at twenty-one miles an hour toward the *Flyer*, in place at the end of a sixty-foot monorail track. At a signal from Orville, the rope holding the *Flyer* was unfastened. The craft was driven by its propellors slowly, then faster, down the track. Wilbur ran alongside it. Orville pulled back the control stick and the wobbly plane rose into the air a few yards. One second . . . three seconds . . . finally twelve seconds it stayed aloft, flying 120 feet until it settled safely to the ground. Men had flown, at last!

Three more times that day, with the brothers taking turns, the *Flyer* went aloft, a little farther each time as the Wrights learned the tricks of controlling it. The fourth flight lasted fifty-nine seconds, covering 852 feet.

Difficult as it is to believe, this achievement that changed the course of the world received little attention. The brothers sent a telegram to their father in Dayton announcing the news. He released the information to a Dayton newspaper, which didn't consider it worth publishing. Some newspapers which learned of the flights from another source published small stories but many, including some of the country's largest, didn't. They and their readers had been so disillusioned by the famous Langley's second failure a few days earlier that they wouldn't believe two unknowns had been successful. Instead of the one to ten million years the New York *Times* had said would be needed, the Wrights succeeded in only two months.

As a sidelight, fifty years later the author of this book, while a newspaper editor in Los Angeles, helped to "rediscover" Charles Taylor, the man who built the engine. He was living as a very old

The first flight by the Wright brothers received little attention. Many newspapers didn't report it at all, others in tiny space. This typical story was published in the South Bend Tribune *with great exaggeration of the distance flown.*

AIRSHIP THAT REALLY FLIES

Dayton Men Successful in Trial at Kitty Hawk, N. C.

Norfolk, Va., Dec. 18.—A successful trial of a flying machine was made yesterday near Kitty Hawk, N. C., by Wilbur and Orville Wright, of Dayton, O. The machine flew for three miles in the face of a wind blowing at the registered velocity of 21 miles an hour and gracefully descended to earth at the spot selected by the man in the navigator's car as a suitable landing place. The machine has no balloon attachment but gets its force from propellers worked by a small engine.

Orville Wright

man in Los Angeles, forgotten in a nursing home. When it learned to its surprise that Taylor was still alive, the aircraft industry honored and assisted him in his final years.

Visitors to the historic scene at Kitty Hawk are impressed by how short man's first flight was, less than half the length of a football field. The National Park Service has reconstructed the

Wilbur Wright

Wrights' 1903 camp. A boulder stands at the precise spot where that first airplane left the ground, and small markers indicate how far each flight went. Standing at this historic site in the dunes and comparing the first tiny plane to the air giants of today is inspiring. A visitors' center nearby contains a replica of the *Flyer* and other material explaining its flight. The actual original Wright brothers' plane is on display at the National Air and Space Museum in Washington.

At first, after the Wrights' invention, hardly anyone else tried

Would-be aviators built airplanes in barns and stables during the years following the Wright brothers' historic flight. This one crashed on its first takeoff attempt and never flew.

to fly. A few improvements were made in the next few years by the Wrights and by Glenn Curtiss, a motorcycle racer who became their competitor in building planes, as well as by flight pioneers in France and England. The pilot began to sit upright instead of lying flat. Landing gear made from bicycle wheels replaced landing skids.

Only a few hundred Americans saw an airplane in the first half dozen years. Then, as the planes became stronger in construction and the early daredevil pilots more skillful, the nation became enchanted with the wonders of flight. Thousands of dollars in

French aviator René Simon toured the Midwest with his Bleriot monoplane in 1911, giving exhibition flights. The pilot even did figure eights in it.

prizes were offered for first flights between various destinations. Air shows were held, to which the curious flocked to gaze at those marvelous new flying machines. Many of the planes tested at these shows failed to fly at all, but some flew at the fantastic speed of sixty miles per hour—a mile a minute!

Soon a star performer emerged, the most daring and romantic early-day pilot of them all. His name was Lincoln Beachey.

Lincoln was a cocky young fellow, short, with a jutting jaw. His first flying shortly after 1900 was done in crude small dirigibles, gas bags with motors. He landed one of them on the lawn of the White House and paid a call on President Theodore Roosevelt's wife. Security precautions at the presidential mansion didn't amount to much in those days. During the air show at Dominguez Field near Los Angeles in 1910, Beachey piloted his balloon in a race against an airplane around the racetrack course, about a hundred feet above the ground. The airplane won. That led

Glenn Curtiss winning speed contest and a $3,000 prize in one of his

Beachey to quit airships and switch to planes. He wasn't the kind of fellow willing to be beaten by anyone or anything.

Soon he was flying a Curtiss pusher biplane and thrilling large crowds, usually at racetracks. The plane was an uncovered wooden frame with the engine and propellor behind the pilot, who sat exposed out front, his feet resting on a bar. Next to him was a seat for a passenger, without a safety strap.

A partner of Beachey's in the early days was Grover Bell, who also had a Curtiss pusher plane. Grover's younger brother Larry went to work for Grover and Beachey as a mechanic at eighteen after graduating from high school. Grover was killed in the crash of his plane not long afterward, but Larry stayed in the airplane business all his life. The world knew him later as Lawrence D. Bell, founder of the Bell Aircraft Corporation that built World War II P-39 fighter planes, Bell helicopters, and the Bell X-1, the first aircraft to fly faster than the speed of sound.

own planes at the Dominguez Air Show near Los Angeles in 1910.

Grover Bell, one of the earliest flyers, sits at the wheel of a plane he owned jointly with his younger brother Lawrence, standing at left, in 1912. Grover was killed when the plane crashed a short time later. Lawrence became the president of Bell Aircraft Corporation.

In his rickety craft, Beachey performed spectacular tricks, seemingly without fear. One of his favorites was flying without hands on the controls—"Look, Ma, no hands!" He took the plane up to five thousand feet, put it into a dive, and with the wind whistling through the reinforcing wires dove toward the ground. He called it the "death dip." Many spectators screamed, sure he was about to crash. Women fainted. At the last second, he leveled off the plane and zoomed down the racetrack straightaway a few feet above the ground.

"Look, he isn't even steering it!" someone exclaimed.

Indeed, he wasn't. He was holding his hands outstretched at his side.

How did he do it? What the crowds didn't know was that in this primitive pusher plane, the banking of the wings was controlled by a yoke attached around the pilot's body. By leaning in a carefully calculated way and by gripping the steering column between his legs, Beachey was able to steer his plane. Unfortunately, other less skillful pilots who tried to imitate this and other Beachey stunts fell to their deaths.

Later on, pilots cut dashing figures in long leather coats, leather helmets, boots, and goggles. That wasn't Beachey's style. While performing his stunts, he wore a dark business suit, a high starched collar, and a necktie with a diamond stickpin—a fashion plate suspended windblown in space. He wore a checkered golf cap, turned backward so the wind wouldn't blow it off during a ninety-mile-an-hour dive.

After a demonstration, Beachey parked his plane near the stands and allowed the admiring crowds to inspect it. A sign warned, "Do not touch." A California friend of this writer remembers how he was taken as a small boy to see the Beachey plane. He was so excited that he disobeyed the sign and touched the canvas-covered wing. His conscience hurt him for days afterward, for fear that by touching the plane secretly he had damaged it and Beachey might crash.

Beachey was willing to fly that plane almost anywhere a crowd could gather, even inside a building. Once in 1913 he took off inside the Machinery Palace on the Exposition grounds at San Francisco, got the plane airborne at sixty miles an hour, and landed it, still inside the hall. He hadn't figured on the floor's being wet, however. The single brake on the front landing wheel wasn't strong enough, and the craft smashed into the far wall. The tense crowd gasped, then fell silent. As Beachey climbed from the damaged plane unhurt, cheers shook the building.

Lincoln Beachey

Another of the stunts that made him famous was matching his airplane against racing automobiles around outdoor tracks. His chief competitors were Barney Oldfield, most popular of the early auto racers, and Eddie Rickenbacker, who later won renown as an American ace fighter pilot in World War I. Beachey flew his plane only a few yards above the race car as the vehicles circled around and around the dirt ovals, about a mile a minute. Usually it was almost an even match.

Perhaps the exploit that brought Beachey the most attention was his flight through Niagara Falls. A throng of 150,000 spectators lined both banks of the gorge below the great waterfall to see him tempt death. Beachey flew his plane at two thousand feet down the Niagara River from Buffalo until he reached the brink of the American Falls, where the torrent plunges over the rock precipice into the gorge below in a cloud of mist. Circling twice, the pilot pointed the plane over the falls and down into the mist. For moments, the crowd saw nothing. Then plane and pilot emerged from the cloud safely, close to the water surface below the falls. Beachey in his dress-up clothing was drenched. Immediately ahead was the bridge between the United States and

Lincoln Beachey in a Curtiss plane races the famous driver Barney Oldfield around a racetrack at about 50 miles per hour. The automobile often won such races because it could make shorter turns.

Canada. The opening under the bridge was only 168 feet high and about a hundred feet wide. Without hesitation, Beachey flew through this small gap and nosed his aircraft up from the gorge toward the Canadian shore. The dripping, coughing plane had just enough power to clear the bluff with a few feet to spare and land intact. Even Beachey must have been a little shaken by the flight; at least he called it the most thrilling of his career and never tried it again.

Although he was collecting big money and ardent cheers, he decided to quit. Bitterly he said, "I am convinced that the only thing that draws crowds to see me is the morbid desire to see something happen. They call me the 'Master Birdman,' but they pay to see me die."

His retirement didn't last long. In 1913, Beachey learned that a French pilot, Adolphe Pégoud, had looped the loop, a spectacular aerial somersault in which the pilot flew a vertical circle by diving, turning back up until he was flying upside down, and leveling off again. Until then, nobody had flown a plane upside down. Before Pégoud tried to perform the stunt, he had his plane slung upside down on trestles on the ground. He was strapped in head downward and practiced working the controls, to determine whether a human could function with the blood rushing to his head.

The challenge was too much for Beachey to ignore. He took to the sky again, mastered the trick of looping in a new plane, and barnstormed around the country doing the loop. The crowds paid heavily for the privilege of being frightened by this newest daredeviltry. Beachey charged $500 for the first loop he did in each city and $200 for each additional. On days when he did six loops, not unusual for him, he was making $1500 for only two or three hours' work, a wonderful way to get rich if you didn't get killed doing it.

Eventually Lincoln Beachey's luck ran out. He had tempted fate successfully thousands of times, but like many less skilled aviators he tried once too often. A crowd of fifty thousand had gathered at the Exposition grounds in San Francisco on March 14, 1915, to see him perform acrobatics in a fast new plane. He gave

A festive group dedicates the speedy new plane of Lincoln Beachey with a bottle of champagne. Beachey, who stands at the right in plaid cap, later crashed in the plane and was killed.

Rear view of the plane in which Lincoln Beachey crashed while stunting. It was considered the sleekest craft in the American skies in 1915. Notice the name Beachey upside down on the top wing.

them a lively show of loops, then began a spectacular vertical letter S maneuver. As he tipped the plane into a steep dive, it went out of control. One wing collapsed up against the side of the plane, then the other. The craft plunged into San Francisco Bay and sank, carrying Beachey to his death. Even the greatest of flyers could not survive when his plane failed.

Beachey's death increased the complaints of newspaper and magazine editors against stunt flying. They lamented the manner in which "sensation-loving mobs" gathered to watch the aviators. Dangerous toys, they called the planes. The editor of *Outlook* condemned stunt flying as morally, if not legally, wrong.

While Beachey and other exhibition flyers excited the public, some far-sighted writers began talking about the day when planes would be carriers of several passengers, perhaps all the way from New York to Philadelphia nonstop.

One national magazine, *Cosmopolitan*, in 1911 thought that the startling sixty-mile-an-hour speed the stunt planes were flying was too perilous and unnecessary. Thirty-five to forty miles an hour was fast enough for passenger planes, it said. Just where to put passengers was a problem. The magazine proposed that they be carried in individual narrow torpedo-like shells suspended between the upper and lower wings of biplanes, to reduce wind resistance. Each of these shells should be of artificial mica, transparent so the passenger could see out in all directions. The writers admitted that these cubicles might be a little cramped. The idea of a closed-in fuselage behind the pilot didn't occur to them.

Cosmopolitan assured would-be passengers that talk about holes in the sky wasn't true. A popular belief held that planes might fly into these mysterious "holes" and plummet to earth. The magazine explained what really happened was that if a plane flying its normal speed of thirty-eight miles an hour encountered a ten-mile-an-hour gust of headwind, the plane lost air speed and its nose dipped down.

If planes ever were to be passenger carriers, they had to be able to fly long distances. Among the prizes posted for aviators was $10,000 by the New York *World* for the first birdman to fly from Albany, New York, to New York City, 152 miles down the

The engine of this plane piloted by Grover Bell in 1912 developed only forty horsepower. Note the pusher propellor behind the engine.

A closeup of a plane Glenn Curtiss built and flew in 1910, with Curtiss standing beside it

Glenn Curtiss

Hudson River. Glenn Curtiss in a pusher plane took off from the state capital in 1910 in pursuit of this prize. A special train carrying officials and newspaper reporters left Albany at the same time on the New York Central tracks down the eastern bank of the Hudson. For a time, train and plane traveled head to head. Passengers leaned from the train windows, waving handkerchieves and scarves at Curtiss above their heads. Slowly the airplane pulled ahead. Twice the pilot had to land for gasoline and oil, but he circled the Statue of Liberty and landed on Governor's Island off Manhattan after nearly three hours in the air, averaging fifty-two miles an hour, and collected the $10,000. His achievement impressed the country so much that the New York *Times* used four and a half pages to cover every detail of the flight.

The greatest prize of all awaited the first aviator to fly across the United States from Atlantic Ocean to Pacific Ocean, or in the other direction. Newspaper publisher William Randolph Hearst offered $50,000 in 1911 for the first transcontinental flight, providing that the pilot completed his trip in thirty days or less.

This sounds absurdly simple today, when hundreds of persons make the journey every day in barely five hours, but in those pioneer days of flight the obstacles were tremendous. No airports existed beyond a few rough fields. Many persons in rural areas had never seen an airplane. The pilots had neither maps nor reliable compasses. There were no paved highways to follow. The surest course for the pilots was to fly along railroad tracks. Their flimsy planes carried enough fuel only for short hops.

Eight men signed up to seek the $50,000. A few never got their planes off the ground. Others started but gave up. One who took off from New York City, intending to follow a railroad west, chose the wrong track out of the complex mass of rails in the New Jersey freight yards and became lost. The man who was the first person to complete a transcontinental flight, Cal Rodgers, took so long to do it that he was disqualified for exceeding the thirty-day limit.

In fact, that first complete transcontinental flight required eighty-four days to reach the Pacific from New York!

Rodgers flew in a Wright biplane with two pusher propellors. From his open seat on the lower wing, he could reach over to his left and touch the little thirty-five horsepower engine. His top speed was fifty-five miles an hour. Cal loved to smoke cigars. Even in the unprotected pilot's seat up in the sky he often puffed away, although he had trouble keeping the cigar lit in a headwind.

On his flight he was accompanied by a special railroad train. This contained spare parts, sleeping quarters, and a repair crew. One car was painted white, so Cal could distinguish his train from the air. To pay for this expensive arrangement, he became a flying advertisement for a grape soft drink called Vin Fiz. Its

Cal Rodgers

maker promised to pay him five dollars for every mile he flew with advertisements for Vin Fiz on the wings and tail. Naturally he called his flying billboard the *Vin Fiz Flyer*.

It is hard to believe all the things that went wrong on Cal's flight. Altogether, he had five crashes so bad that his plane had to be almost entirely rebuilt, and seven lesser ones. Repeatedly his engine sputtered and died in flight. Once a hose connection broke while he was flying and splattered hot water on him. Another time, he crashed into a chicken coop. When a spark plug fell out of the engine on one hop, Rodgers coolly reached over and held it in place while continuing to fly.

Cal Rodgers simply wouldn't quit. On his best days he flew two hundred miles. At times he was grounded for days. His passage over towns at low altitude and overnight stops caused a sensation. The day after he stopped at Hammond, Indiana, a nine-year-old boy tried to imitate him by building a plane from pieces of wood, sheets, and his mother's clothesline. The steering wheel was taken from the family washing machine. While his mother was away, he pulled the "plane" onto the roof of the barn and pushed off in it. His mother found him unconscious on the ground in the debris when she returned home.

Cal Rodgers in cap stands in front of the plane in which he made the first flight across the United States in 1911.

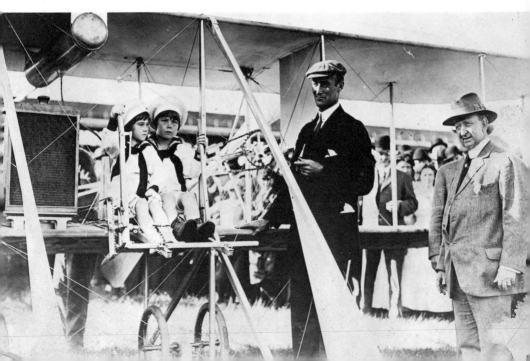

After three weeks, Rodgers reached Chicago. Kansas City closed its schools so the students could watch him fly over. A newspaper in Muskogee, Oklahoma, commented, "To those who saw Rodgers alight and step from his machine, there came a sensation as if they had just seen a messenger from Mars." A messenger puffing a cigar, it might have added.

Finally, after forty-nine days, Cal Rodgers landed the *Vin Fiz Flyer* in Pasadena, California, ten miles northeast of Los Angeles. A cheering crowd greeted him with flowers, and his admirers wrapped him in an American flag. He still wasn't satisfied. Coast-to-coast meant all the way to the Pacific Ocean. A flight of about thirty miles remained to the water's edge at Long Beach.

Even on this final stretch, he couldn't shake his bad luck. About halfway, he was forced to make an emergency crash landing at Compton in which he damaged the plane severely and broke his

When Cal Rodgers finally reached Pasadena, California, from New York after a flight of forty-nine days, his welcomers wrapped him in an American flag.

Early-day airplanes took off from and landed on narrow beaches at the edge of the Pacific Ocean, as lines of spectators watched. Bicycle wheels formed the landing gear.

ankle. Another month passed until he could hobble on crutches to the rebuilt plane and fly it to Long Beach. With his crutches stowed on the wing beside him and a big grin surrounding his cigar, he taxied the *Vin Fiz Flyer* across the sand until the waves of the Pacific dampened the bicycle tires of his landing gear.

Eighty-four days, but he made it! Aviation took a great stride forward that day.

— 3 —

Those Crazy Barnstormers

When old-time aviators tell stories about their adventures, the yarn spinning is called "hangar flying." After their planes are parked safely in the hangar, they get to talking and soon are recounting tales of daring and luck in the air.

Some of their memories about the early days of flying are so vivid that they may seem hard to believe: of men without parachutes hanging by their toes from rope ladders under planes . . . a woman dropping from a low-flying plane onto a moving train . . . a wingwalker jumping from a plane without a parachute and landing safely. Hangar flying does tend to make stories grow bigger as they are repeated, but the truth about aviation in the "barnstorming" days is so fascinating that it doesn't need exaggerations to intrigue us.

Many young American men had their first taste of flying during World War I. The United States sent some aviators to the battlefields of France and was training more when the war ended on November 11, 1918. Airplanes had been improved during the war and began to look more like those with which we are familiar today—at least the small sports planes we see around private airports. Quite a few of the men who had a taste of flying during the war didn't want to quit it after the Armistice. So they went into barnstorming.

Barnstorming meant buying a second-hand military plane for about $300 and touring around the country with it, stopping in

Hanging beneath the airplane, this wingwalker has nothing to keep him from falling if he loosens his grip.

each town for a few days to take passengers for rides—usually the first time the customers had been in the air—and building up the townspeople's interest with stunt flying. The more the barnstorming pilots could make 'em gasp, the more the crowds admired their skill and felt safe enough to risk their own lives on fifteen-minute flights. Usually the fee for a passenger was $15.00 for a quarter-hour ride, a dollar a minute, and $25.00 if the pilot tossed in a few maneuvers like a spin or even a loop. These barnstorming days of the 1920's provided the introduction of thousands of Americans, especially those who lived in small towns, to airplanes. From the cow-pasture barnstormers, ready to land their planes anywhere and fly them under all sorts of conditions, came many of the later leaders of the aircraft industry, airline pilots, and World War II military heroes.

Mostly the barnstormers flew Curtiss Jennies. The Jenny was known officially during World War I as the JN-4D, but everyone knew her by the nickname. She was a biplane whose top wing was forty-three feet wide and lower wing considerably shorter.

The two open seats in the fuselage were one behind the other, behind the engine. Usually the pilot sat in the rear cockpit, the passenger up front. The Jenny was rugged, and today she seems laughably slow. On a calm day she could fly at seventy-five miles an hour. She could land at forty-five miles an hour. Many times when the motor failed in flight, the pilot brought his Jenny to a safe dead-stick landing, coasting into the smoothest-looking field available with no power at all.

A Jenny could land or take off from almost any pasture that wasn't cluttered with trees or fences. The cows in the field usually trotted out of the way when they heard the noise of the engine and the *whirr* of the wooden propellor. Occasionally one didn't move fast enough, resulting in disaster for the cow or the plane, or both. Once a Jenny got into the air, climbing took a long time, five minutes to rise to an altitude of one thousand feet. This meant that most barnstorming was done at low altitude. The Jenny's fuel tank held only twenty-one gallons, so when barnstormers set up shop in a field outside a town and their passenger-ride business

One of the famous Jenny biplanes, surplus aircraft from World War I that were used by many barnstormers. Notice the military number still visible under the newly painted civilian 14.

Small-town boys admire barnstormers and their Jenny in a pasture at the edge of town, while a businessman poses proudly with them.

Barnstormers used newspaper advertisements like this to attract passengers.

was brisk, they had to keep an errand boy running into town for more fuel.

Some of the pilots flew a variation of the Jenny with shorter wings, the JN-4C, called a Canuck. Often the barnstormers carried blanket rolls in their cockpits and slept on the ground under the wing of the plane, to protect it and to save money on hotel bills. Few flyers got rich from barnstorming, although they had fun and felt delightfully carefree.

What was it like, taking your first flight in one of these open cockpit planes? When two barnstormers came to South Bend, Indiana, in the summer of 1919, giving residents of that city their first opportunity to fly, they invited a newspaper reporter up for a ride. They figured that his story would whet his readers' desire

55

to try the sky. It did, too. And the daily newspapers dutifully published the names of all the townspeople who had the nerve and the $15.00 to take a ride.

Outfitted in leather helmet and goggles, the reporter climbed onto the lower wing of the Jenny, then into the front cockpit. Here is how he described the takeoff:

"The first thrill is in getting a close view of the machine itself. To see the bright wings, the powerful motor, and effective balancing apparatus there in front of you—not up in the air but where you can see all the details—and to realize that this machine is to bear you up among the clouds, or close to them, at least, sets your heart beating a trifle faster.

"Then you climb in. The novelty of the situation is another thrill. You're not in an automobile, for the sides of the fuselage come up to your shoulders and you have to be buckled in, so that you can't fall out.

"The motor starts, the machine vibrates just a little. 'I'll be in the air in a minute!' you think.

"In a moment, the plane begins its run for the takeoff. The wheels rumble over the rough ground, and the wind sings in your ears. The motor roars. You feel an invisible hand lifting you up, gently at first, then more rapidly. You're flying! Oh, thrills!"

How different this is from taking off today in an airliner from a big terminal. The passenger walks through a movable loading tunnel directly into the jetliner's cabin, sits in a soft armed seat, watches a uniformed stewardess point to the emergency exits and other features of the spacious cabin, and listens to piped-in music. As the plane gathers speed down the broad concrete runway, the traveler barely realizes that the craft carrying perhaps two hundred persons has left the ground and is pointed sharply upward toward thirty thousand feet.

Despite the comforts and safety of flight in a modern airliner, the men who barnstormed in the slowpoke Jennies could do things with them that are impossible now. Can you imagine the captain of a gigantic 747 climbing from his seat onto the top of

This midwestern attorney enjoyed his first airplane ride, in this Jenny owned by two barnstormers, so much that his wife took one, too. She replaced her broad hat with a helmet.

What a place to stand on your head—on top of an airplane engine hundreds of feet in the air, without a parachute!

the plane in flight, crawling back to the tail, and piloting the plane from that rear position by manipulating the controls with his hands and feet? With nobody in the cockpit at all? Barnstorming stunt flyers did that in their Jennies. Without parachutes, at that!

These flyers truly were daredevils. They tried to top each other with midair stunts that grew constantly zanier and more frightening to the audiences down below. Although many of them died in crashes or falls when they pushed the law of gravity too far, the tragedies didn't stop others. The crazier the stunts were, the larger the crowds they attracted to the air circuses the traveling aviators staged in town after town, and the more the flyers earned.

As an example, the two young barnstormers in whose Jenny that awestruck reporter rode did stunts over the downtown shopping district of the city at an altitude of only one thousand feet. The co-pilot climbed from his cockpit onto the top of the fuselage, crept to the tail, stood upright without hanging onto anything and waved to the gawking spectators. Once he was back in the cockpit, the pilot set a course right along the city's main street. He flew upside down and did a series of low-level loop-the-loops, barrel rolls, wingovers, and other maneuvers. To climax the performance he climbed a bit higher, let the Jenny stall into a tailspin, and leveled her off safely a few hundred feet above the spectators' heads.

Even more startling was the feat by some trick flyers of doing a loop with a man standing on the top wing, even while the plane was flying upside down at the top of the circle. The wing man was held in place by guy wires invisible from the ground.

Some stunts were less dangerous than they appeared from the ground because of secret safety devices. The trick of a man hanging by his teeth from a leather strap suspended below the landing gear was an example. This thrilled and frightened the crowds looking up, who believed that if the daredevil's jaw tired he would fall to his death. They didn't know that he had a thin steel cable fastened from the landing gear crossbar to a strong harness under his flying coat.

Today's sleek planes are too swift and too streamlined for use in this kind of stunting. They can't fly slowly enough for anyone to climb around on a wing in flight and survive; the wind pressure

A stunt man hangs by his teeth from a rope ladder suspended from an airplane.

"Taking the hat" was a popular stunt at early-day air shows. Here two men hanging by one hand to the wing tips of the low-flying plane grab hats held out to them as the plane speeds past.

Airplane motors have changed greatly since this picture was taken in 1919, and so has the clothing of girls who gather to look at them.

is too great. Enclosed cockpits, retractable landing gear that folds into the fuselage during flight, and the disappearance of wing struts and guy wires have eliminated the handholds and footrests so essential for stunting. Planes now are built for speed and efficiency, not for circus-like fun.

One veteran of those barnstorming days recalled later how he had soloed at the age of twelve in a Jenny, without intending to do so. Flying was that casual then. While a boy in Corpus Christi,

Some early airplanes had three wings. This Catron and Fisk design flew in 1921.

Texas, in 1921, J.O. Dockery was hired by a man selling surplus World War I planes to guard them. As a reward, he was taken on a ten-hour aerial tour of Texas during which he followed closely everything the pilot did, putting his hands on the dual controls. Shortly thereafter, the pilot-salesman went away on another trip, leaving the twelve-year-old guard on duty.

Nobody was around, and Dockery, an adventurous boy, was curious. What would it be like, sitting in the pilot's cockpit and pretending to fly? He climbed into the cockpit and got the engine

61

In this first midair refueling, a wingwalker with a five-gallon can of gasoline strapped on his back climbs from the lower plane to the upper one and pours the fuel into its tank.

started. With no one to stop him, he taxied the plane across the bumpy field. He was light and the gas tank was almost empty. The plane gathered momentum. Suddenly the boy found himself flying level with the treetops. He had taken off without really trying to do so! Fortunately, he knew enough to get the Jenny back to earth safely. Fifty years later he was still talking about his surprise.

Changing from one plane to another while high in the air was a favorite crowd-pleaser in the air circuses. Spectators watched tensely as two biplanes drew alongside, wing tip to wing tip, and a man or woman stunt performer—yes, there were a few women barnstormers—jumped from one plane to the other. Even that wasn't risky enough for one stunt performer. He changed planes with one hand tied behind his back!

Today, refueling of long range military planes in midair by tanker plane has been developed into an intricate art. The first known midair refueling back in the 1920's was a haphazard stunt in a Jenny.

A pilot named Earl Daugherty announced that he intended to keep his Jenny aloft for twenty-four hours. It was obvious that the Jenny couldn't carry enough gasoline for that, but Daugherty took off, anyway, at the Long Beach Airport in California. Just when his fuel tank was nearing the empty mark, another biplane drew alongside. Standing on the top wing was a wingwalker, Wesley May. Strapped on May's back was a five-gallon can of gasoline. When the planes were almost touching, May stepped over onto Daugherty's wing, walked across it to the engine, and poured gasoline into the tank.

Since these traveling shows always needed fresh ways to thrill the crowds and sell tickets, the pilots were kept busy concocting new stunts. A parachute jump was a standard part of air shows. The audiences loved to see a man jump from a plane, then a few seconds later see his parachute billow open and float him safely to earth right in front of them. This led one crew of barnstormers to announce plans for a man to leap from an airplane without a parachute. He did so, too, and survived.

While the biplane flew over the crowd, the jumper climbed from his cockpit down onto the undercarriage, where he swung

Three daredevil wingwalkers perform simultaneously on the top wing of a Jenny in the air above Los Angeles.

by his knees on the crossbar that connected the two landing wheels. He had no parachute. The pilot flew low and as slowly as his plane would go without stalling. At the agreed moment, the man on the undercarriage let go and fell—right into a haystack!

Another pilot with a gruesome sense of humor terrified a crowd by putting his plane into a loop. While flying upside down, he pushed out of the cockpit the dummy of a man dressed like an aviator. The crowd saw the body falling. No parachute opened. Gasps came from the stands, then cries of distress as the "aviator" crumbled onto the field before the terrified eyes of the spectators. The crowd swept onto the field, running to see if the man was dead, as he must be. Before any of them could reach him, however, an ambulance drove up, the crew placed him inside, and the vehicle sped away. Not until later was the crowd told that the "victim" was a dummy. In defense of this dubious jest, the flyers responsible pointed out that many in the crowd probably had a

An amusement park crowd in California in 1920 watches pilot Earl Daugherty fly past with a stunt man standing on the upper wing. Such demonstrations of daring drew large audiences.

Jimmy Doolittle, after he led the American bomber raid on Tokyo in 1942, and by Milton Caniff, courtesy Aviation Hall of Fame.

secret desire to see a plane crash or someone killed. This way they attained their desire without anyone's being really hurt.

Jimmy Doolittle was one of the pilots who tested his nerve and learned the tricks of flying during the barnstorming era, then went on to world fame. As Lieutenant Colonel Doolittle in World War II, he led the squadron of American bombers that took off from an aircraft carrier in the Pacific Ocean and bombed Tokyo. The raid startled the Japanese. Taking place early in the war, when the enemy was winning after its sneak attack on Pearl Harbor, the Doolittle raid gave Americans hope and confidence.

For Doolittle and his raiders, the risks were tremendous. But that was the way Jimmy had flown since the early days, calculating the risks and then taking them. Unlike most of the barnstormers, he stayed in the United States Army after being a cadet in the first world war and did most of his flying in military planes.

By the end of World War II, he was a three-star lieutenant general and one of his country's most admired aerial heroes.

As a young aviator, Doolittle loved speed and pranks. He became the first pilot to fly across the United States in less than twenty-four hours. That was in 1922, only eleven years after Cal Rodgers required eighty-four days for the same transcontinental flight, an indication of how swiftly aviation was developing. Doolittle later set many other speed records.

One of his jokes took place when he was flying an unusual high-winged monoplane in an air show. He attached an extra landing gear upside down on top of the wing and a dummy head projecting underneath the fuselage. Then he flew past the crowd upside down, leaving them baffled. A pilot's head and landing gear appeared both on the top and bottom of the plane. Which side was up?

The craziest stunt flyers of all were those who performed in the silent motion pictures. Movies still were something of a novelty in the early 1920's, photographed only in black and white. The villains leered and the heroines sighed heavily, with elaborate facial expressions and waving of the arms in place of spoken words. Theater-goers paid fifteen or twenty cents to see a show, and they

A stunt man climbs from an automobile up a rope ladder into a passing airplane. The vehicles were moving about fifty miles an hour.

demanded action, the wilder the better. The movie stunt men provided it.

Script writers and the pilots themselves cooked up aerial adventures so bizarre that even the most foolhardy of the "I'll-try-anything-once" flyers had trouble pulling them off. Many of the wildest took place in the Saturday afternoon serials. Week after week, the heroine or hero was maneuvered into a seemingly impossible position as the episode ended, about to be pushed over a cliff or run over by a train while held down in some form by the villain. At the next Saturday matinee, the movie house was full of boys and girls (and adults, too) anxious to see how the "good guy" escaped. Everybody knew he or she would, impossible as it seemed.

One of these serials starring Ruth Roland was built around a wacky airplane sequence. The heroine in distress was shown in an open automobile, trying to escape the "bad guys." She had a wireless transmitter, with which she called an aviator to rescue her. A low-flying biplane appeared overhead with a rope ladder dangling. Ruth reached up, grabbed the rope, and climbed hand over hand to the plane. The plane passed low over a speeding passenger train on a nearby track, and Ruth descended the ladder, dropping onto the roof of the train. She crawled into the passenger coach and had a gunfight with one of the villains. Back up to the train roof she went, grabbed the ladder beneath the plane, and once more climbed up to the cockpit. The plane flew back over her automobile, and the heroine scrambled down into the driver's seat. She drove away in a cloud of dust with the bad guys in close pursuit. In the closing scene, the heroine raced her automobile across the track just ahead of the train. The villains' car a few feet behind was struck broadside by the train. Justice was done! How much more action could a movie fan want? The precision flying required to make this wild sequence work was superb, even though the story was ridiculous.

Best known of the movie stunt pilots was a cool-nerved fellow named Frank Clarke. He seemed to be entirely without fear. Once he and a partner, Mark Campbell, went up together in a biplane with the movie cameraman in another craft flying alongside. Clarke

After climbing all over the plane, a cool-nerved wingwalker without parachute waves from the top wing of Frank Clarke's Jenny to the crowds hundreds of feet below.

was dressed as a policeman, Campbell in the prison stripes of a convict. Campbell climbed onto a wing. Clarke, the pilot, got out of his cockpit in pursuit of the "criminal." The two chased each other all over the plane, from one wing to the other and back onto the fuselage. The plane flew on with nobody at the controls (Clarke had tied them in place with a rope). The shifting weight of the men made the plane rock. Finally, the policeman caught his man by crawling from the lower wing down through the undercarriage that supported the wheels and back up onto the wing on the other side. Neither actor had a parachute. Sheer foolhardy craziness, of course, but how the film audiences loved it!

Souvenir hunters were a constant problem to the barnstormers. If they weren't careful, visitors would steal pieces of the parked airplanes, even the few instruments they had in the cockpits. Once while barnstorming Clarke used a unique way to prevent such

Wingwalker Leigh Sellers thrills crowd below by crawling back from the cockpit and standing up on the plane's tail, without benefit of a parachute.

theft. He borrowed a rattlesnake from a friend who ran an animal show. When Clarke left his plane unattended, he removed the rattlesnake from its box and turned it loose in the cockpit. If a souvenir hunter came close, the angered snake sounded his ominous rattles and the would-be thief scurried away.

There was almost no end to the spectacular stunts and variations Clarke performed in front of the cameras during his long and amazingly lucky career. Wing-walking was common practice; Clarke added a touch by walking out on the lower wing in flight while handcuffed. He almost fell to his death when his foot slipped. Forgetting that his wrists were bound together by steel cuffs, he reached for one of the reinforcing wires that ran between the upper and lower wings. He missed it and was blown backward, only to fall against another wire just before being swept off into space. Another time, as he rode a horse across a field, a biplane flew past just barely above the ground as it took off. Clarke jumped from the horse onto the tail of the plane and climbed up into the second cockpit.

As his use of the snake indicates, he was quite a practical joker. He took two motion picture friends aloft one day for what they thought was to be a quiet sight-seeing tour. The two guests were crowded together in the front cockpit, Clarke piloting from the rear one. While cruising along, he slid down from his seat onto the floor of the cockpit, out of sight. In those old biplanes, the control wires were strung along the bottom of the fuselage, so Clarke could steer by pulling the wires with his hands, even though he could not see ahead. He put the plane in a steep dive, then pulled its nose up suddenly. He did it again. This was more than his landlubber friends had bargained for. One turned around to protest—and gasped. There was no pilot in the rear cockpit! The passengers were terrified. Neither could fly, and there were no controls in the front cockpit even if they could.

Suddenly, the plane went into a spin and twisted toward earth out of control. The passengers, sensing that they were doomed, braced themselves for the crash. But it didn't come. Gradually the plane righted itself. They looked around once more, and there was Clarke calmly sitting in the pilot's seat, bringing them in for a smooth landing. Somehow, Clarke thought the joke was much

With no one in the cockpit, the pilot steers this barnstorming plane in the air by pulling control wires from the tail, while his partner hangs from a wing strut.

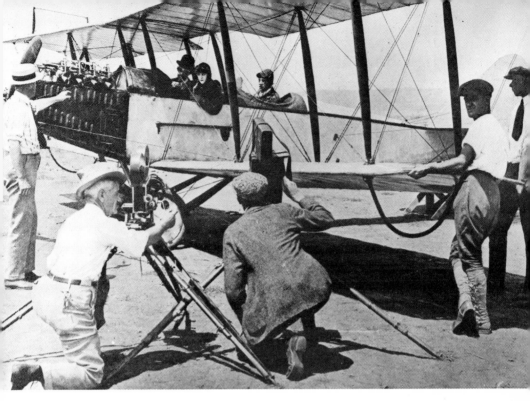

Director Al Christie in straw hat instructs performers during the filming of an airplane scene in the silent movie, He Married His Wife. *By shooting from a low angle, the cameras make the plane appear to be in the air. The man at the wing tip rocks the wing to simulate motion.*

funnier than his guests did.

The daredevil act that brought Frank Clarke the most publicity involved a movie scene in which he, doubling for the hero, made a spectacular rooftop escape by plane. The scene was the roof of a thirteen-story building in downtown Los Angeles. The plot called for the hero to run out on the roof while trying to escape the villains, jump into his airplane, which somehow happened to be waiting for him, and take off from the roof.

Word had spread that the stunt was about to be filmed, and spectators had gathered in the streets below. Such an extremely dangerous feat had never been attempted before. The roof was only ninety-five feet wide; in that tiny distance the plane had to gather enough speed to become airborne. A wooden runway with an incline at the end had been built across the roof, invisible to

71

Daredevil stunt pilot Frank Clarke takes off from the roof of a twelve-story building in downtown Los Angeles in a silent movie thriller.

the crowd below. The incline was intended to give Clark's Jenny a little extra help.

Dressed like the hero and pretending to be him, Clarke ran onto the roof, roared the Jenny's motor, gave a signal to the cameraman, and took off along the all-too-short runway. As it hit the incline, the plane bounced into the air over the roof edge. Clarke dipped its nose to gather momentum, leveled off two or three stories above the ground and waggled his wings in a victory sign to the cheering crowd as he flew away down a city street. The script writers couldn't get the better of him!

Even Frank Clarke's luck ran out eventually. Like Lincoln Beachey and many other barnstorming men, he died in the crash of his plane. He was more fortunate than most, however, because he flew for more than thirty years through one narrow escape after another. By then, the odds were stacked heavily against him. In 1948, he had gone to pay an aerial call on a friend who owned a mine in the mountains. Clarke saluted the miner with a stunt dive toward the entrance of the mine shaft. He had done identical dives hundreds of times. This time, however, the controls jammed and the plane struck the ground in flames.

The roll of lives lost among these pioneer airmen who did so much to make the mass of Americans air-conscious during the 1920's was long and sad. They lived perilously, usually in a happy-go-lucky way, flying at a time when few government restrictions existed to control their antics. During this period, passenger travel began to develop, and the first organized airlines started operation with only one or two planes. Speed and distance flying began to replace aerial acrobatics in the public's attention.

— 4 —

Around the World

Ever since Christopher Columbus set out to prove that the earth was not flat and travelers would not fall off its edge, the idea of going around the world has fascinated adventurers. Ferdinand Magellan's expedition was the first to do so, requiring three years to circumnavigate the globe in creaky little vessels in 1519-22. French novelist Jules Verne caught the world's fancy with his tale *Around the World in Eighty Days,* in which an Englishman on a wager made the journey by balloon, ship, and train while enduring a series of astounding adventures. To the readers of the 1870's, eighty days was such a short time in which to circle the globe that the trip could be done only in a writer's imagination.

It wasn't surprising, then, that aviators dreamed of flying around the world. Surely they could do so in less time than Verne's imaginary eighty days, if they had a plane capable of crossing wide stretches of ocean. Who would be the first to succeed?

In the early 1920's, the United States Army Air Service did not have much to do. The country was at peace after World War I. Congress gave the Air Service little money. The military airmen believed fervently that airplanes were a crucial tool in the country's armed strength; their problem was to prove this to the government.

Loudest among the airmen trying to convince the old-time generals and admirals that they should pay more attention to aviation was General Billy Mitchell. He argued in 1921 that air-

This twin-motored Martin bomber, photographed in 1919, was one of the United States' few relatively large planes just after World War I. Note the machine guns at the nose and behind the wings.

A helmeted pilot and two friends standing beside a 1919 Martin bomber give an indication of the plane's size, very large for that time.

General Billy Mitchell leads the bombers which sank a captured German battleship in a demonstration of what air power could do against naval vessels.

planes dropping bombs could destroy huge battleships, which were the backbone of the United States Navy. The admirals in command didn't believe it. Neither did a former Assistant Secretary of the Navy, whose name was Franklin D. Roosevelt. He said, "It is highly unlikely that an airplane or fleet of them could ever successfully attack a fleet of Navy vessels under battle conditions."

Grudgingly, the Navy agreed to let Mitchell and his bombers test their theory on a captured German battleship, the *Ostfriesland*. The Navy regarded the vessel as unsinkable. Mitchell's planes practiced on smaller captured vessels, then flew out to attack the battleship in the Atlantic Ocean off Virginia. These aircraft, while larger and stronger than the Jennies the barnstormers used, were fragile and tiny compared to the military planes of today. The biggest of them could carry one 2,000-pound bomb. Six planes flew over the 27,000-ton battleship one at a time. When the fifth bomb hit the water alongside it, the dreadnaught began to go down at the stern. A few minutes later it turned over on its side with a towering splash and sank.

Mitchell had proven his point. Later, he criticized the Army and Navy so vehemently that he was court-martialed. Although he had shown how vulnerable they were, the Navy continued to place heavy dependence on battleships. Twenty years later, in December, 1941, when Roosevelt was President of the United States, squadrons of Japanese bombers attacked the American fleet of battleships and support vessels without warning at Pearl Harbor in the Hawaiian Islands and virtually wiped it out, bringing the United States into World War II. Pearl Harbor was a terrible reminder of the lesson Billy Mitchell had tried to teach his superiors back in 1921.

Next, the Air Service set out to demonstrate how far and how fast military planes could go. A flight by a group of Air Service planes around the world seemed a splendid way to make the point.

That flight did succeed. Six United States Air Service men in three planes flew around the earth in 1924, starting westward from Seattle, Washington, and returning to that city from the east after a series of adventures and mishaps that rivaled Jules Verne's fiction. Instead of breaking the eighty-day record of that author's hero, however, they required 175 days, more than twice as long. They had troubles that even the fanciful French writer didn't dream up. But then, he didn't know about the whims of pioneer airplanes.

General Billy Mitchell inspects a new type of plane with the cockpit enclosed, in the early 1920's.

Four open-cockpit biplanes called World Cruisers, with a top speed of 103 miles per hour, were built especially for this attempt by Donald Douglas. They took off from Seattle on April 6, 1924, each carrying two men. Only two of the four original planes with four men aboard completed the girdling of the globe. The third ended as a pile of debris on a mountainside in Alaska, and the fourth lies at the bottom of the Atlantic. Fortunately, all four men involved in the accidents escaped safely. Two of them, in fact, arrived in Seattle flying a replacement plane but had been forced to travel part way by ship.

The four planes were named to honor American cities—the *Seattle*, the *Chicago*, the *Boston*, and the *New Orleans*. Each was propelled by a single 400-horsepower Liberty engine.

More than 26,000 miles, the length of this flight around the world, was an unheard-of distance for airplanes to fly in the mid-1920's. The Air Service knew that the flight could succeed only if the government made elaborate preparations that included emergency supplies and spare engines at depots along the route. United States Navy destroyers patrolled the ocean areas along the route, ready to rescue any of the aviators if they crashed. By the time the flyers had circled the earth and returned to the takeoff site at Seattle, the World Cruisers had made seventy-three separate flights, visited twenty-nine countries, had five forced landings, and used up seventeen engines. The crews had not been especially anxious to visit all those countries, but their planes were incapable of the long non-stop hops we take for granted today. The capability of the World Cruisers was stretched to the utmost on the longest jump of all, 830 miles across the turbulent North Atlantic from Reykjavik, Iceland, to Frederiksdal, Greenland.

Despite the elaborate preparations, the four planes needed three attempts before they actually got started from Seattle. The first takeoff was canceled because of fog. On the second day, the expedition commander, Major Frederick L. Martin in the *Seattle*, broke a propellor. Even when the trip finally began on the third day, the *Boston*, piloted by Lieutenant Leigh Wade, could not get off the water and had to trail along several hours later.

These special Douglas planes had an unusual feature: they

could use either pontoons or wheels, for water or land takeoffs and landings. Since the first half of the route was up the west coast of Canada, along the Alaskan shore and the Aleutian Islands, then down the coast of Asia to Japan and India, the planes started from Seattle as seaplanes. When the expedition eventually reached Calcutta, India, pontoons were replaced by wheels. In England, pontoons were put on again for the North Atlantic crossing.

When the four planes took off from Seattle in early April, winter still reigned in the Far North. Snow fell heavily as they flew from Canada into Alaska. It drifted into the open cockpits and almost blinded the pilot and mechanic assigned to each aircraft. The plan was for the four to fly in formation, but soon they became separated in the storm. Since the planes had no radios, the only way the pilots could keep in touch with each other was by visual signaling, impossible in the snow.

Later, Lieutenant Erik H. Nelson, pilot of the *New Orleans*, told about this part of the flight: "Sometimes we flew so low that our pontoons almost dragged on the water. Most of the time I flew standing up in the cockpit braced against the back of the seat with my feet on the rudder bar so that I could look out the front of the plane as well as over the side. Every few minutes I had to change goggles because the snow driving against my face melted, trickled down behind them and blurred the lenses."

Bad luck plagued the *Seattle*. While flying along the Alaskan coast, Major Martin noticed that the engine had lost its oil pressure. After he made a forced landing in a cove somewhat protected from the Pacific Ocean waves, he and his mechanic, Sergeant Alva L. Harvey, found that a hole in the crankcase had ruined the engine. They were miles from a settlement. The other planes had gone on ahead, and without a radio the stranded plane could not call for help. Through the whole Arctic night the men shivered in their open cockpits, wondering how they would get help and afraid to risk letting the plane drift in to shore. A destroyer found them the next morning and towed the *Seattle* to a village, where it was pushed up a creek into shelter. Another Navy vessel brought a replacement engine. By the light of a lantern, Sergeant Harvey

This is one of the first American planes to take off from water, in 1912. Grover Bell is at the controls. His 18-year-old brother, Larry, built the pontoon and replaced the plane's wheels with it.

On the first flight around the world, the World Cruiser Chicago is shown here with pontoons. On part of the flight they were replaced by wheels.

and a sailor worked all night installing the fresh engine. When dawn came, the men chopped ice off the pontoons with a hatchet and flew to the tiny Alaskan village of Chignik.

The other three planes were waiting at Dutch Harbor for the *Seattle* to catch up. Before Martin and Harvey could leave Chignik for the reunion at Dutch Harbor, they had to chop and scrape four hundred pounds of ice from the plane's surfaces. Snow swirled around them as they bounced over the choppy sea on takeoff. Having been told about a shortcut, they pointed inland rather than follow the meandering coast. Visibility was almost zero. Unexpectedly, a mountain peak rose out of the mist dead in their course. Martin swerved the plane and sought some way out of their perilous location. The men strained to see what was ahead.

Almost simultaneously they sighted a rocky, treeless ridge of the mountain so close that there was no time to avoid it. The *Seattle* smashed into the mountainside and was demolished. Perhaps because its pontoons cushioned the shock, Martin and Harvey survived without serious injury.

Although still alive, by good luck, their plight was grim enough: lost on a mountainside, shrouded in fog, with scant hope of rescue. If they were to get out alive, they must do so on their own.

They warmed themselves over a fire built from the wooden wing struts and other pieces of the wreck, then huddled for the night in the baggage compartment of the plane, trying to keep each other warm. Since fog still smothered the mountain the next morning, they dared not walk out into the unknown. Instead, they built an igloo from blocks of snow, Eskimo style, and covered the top with canvas from the wings. Here they took shelter for two days, chewing malted milk balls as their only nourishment. When the fog lifted, they climbed the mountain to a crest and in the distance saw water. This gave them a destination, if they could reach it. For two days they stumbled down the mountain to the shore, where luck finally came their way. They found a trapper's cabin stocked with food. By then, Harvey was suffering from snow blindness.

After two days of recuperation, the two aviators walked along

Two views of the U.S. Air Service planes that made the first flight around the world. They are pulled up on foreign beaches for inspection.

the shore, searching for a settlement. The exhausted men were seen by Eskimos in a fishing boat, taken aboard, and carried to a cannery farther along the coast. Martin and Harvey had been missing for eleven days; the world assumed they were dead. When a radio message sent from the remote cannery announced their safe arrival, the news caused elation back in the States.

The disappearance of the command plane and the expedition's leader could not halt the around-the-world attempt. The *Chicago, Boston,* and *New Orleans* flew on from Dutch Harbor while the two crash victims still were missing. Their course was a series of hops from settlement to settlement strung out along the dreary, cloud-shrouded Aleutian Islands which point across the top of the Pacific Ocean toward Asia.

At one native village the six crewmen, awaiting better weather, took shelter in a shut-down trading post. Their food supply consisted of flour and condensed milk, a diet of which they quickly became weary. They looked enviously at a flock of chickens owned by an Aleut resident. Visions of platters heaped with fried chicken ran through their minds.

One morning the Aleut told the flyers that the engine of his motorboat would not start. "Will you fix it?" he asked.

"We will if you will pay us with two chickens."

He agreed.

The mechanics uncrossed the wires in the engine's magneto, and it started immediately. That night the aviators dined on chicken. They knew exactly how to repair the motorboat, since they had crossed the wires the previous night when its owner wasn't near.

Courage and skill weren't the only requirements for long-distance flights in those days. A little ingenuity and scheming helped, too.

When the three surviving planes reached Japan, their welcome was tumultuous. The crewmen found themselves invited to dinners and receptions but had no proper uniforms, since theirs had been left behind to save weight. A destroyer rushed them a new set, so they could represent their country in proper social style.

Another serious mishap overtook the expedition when it was flying over the Gulf of Tonkin, a place that was to become famous during the Vietnam war forty years later. The *Chicago's* engine overheated, and Lieutenants Lowell H. Smith and Leslie P. Arnold were forced to land in a jungle lagoon. An inspection showed the engine to be ruined. All they could do was wait, meanwhile trying to converse with the Vietnamese who swarmed around them, friendly and curious. After the other two planes landed at the next city, their crews arranged for a Navy destroyer to bring a spare engine to Hue from Saigon, other names that American soldiers came to know well in later years. But how to get the crippled *Chicago* from its lagoon resting place to Hue for repairs?

A native village leader solved the problem, although he knew nothing about mechanics. Three war sampans in line, each with ten oarsmen, were hooked to the crippled seaplane. They towed it twenty-five miles in ten hours to Hue while the two aviators reclined on the wings. Wives and girl friends of the paddlers traveled alongside in other boats, reaching over to stuff bits of food into the mouths of the boatmen as they paddled relentlessly ahead—a strange procession of the modern and the ancient in a faraway land. At Hue the *Chicago* was tethered under a bridge, so that the damaged engine could be pulled up from the plane by ropes and a new one lowered into place.

After that, things went well. The World Cruisers advanced by flights of a few hundred miles across India, through the Middle East and southeastern Europe. The aviators landed in Paris for the gala Bastille Day celebration on July 14, exhausted but pleased with their progress. The world seemed a long way around, indeed, but they were getting there. The men were so weary that when they went as guests to the renowned Paris nightlife theater, the Folies-Bergère, some of the men fell asleep during the show. A few nights later in London, one of them dozed off and snored during a formal dinner. His British hosts were too polite to awaken him.

One great obstacle remained, the Atlantic Ocean. A direct flight across it was beyond the capacity of the World Cruisers. So the flyers set off on an island-hopping course in an arc across the upper North Atlantic from the Orkney Islands north of Scotland to Iceland, to Greenland, and then to Labrador, their first point back on North American soil.

The *Boston* was destined not to get home safely. It developed engine trouble on the northbound trip to Iceland that required a forced landing in heavy seas. The two crewmen sat in their cockpits for several hours helplessly, bouncing on the waves, until a British trawler reached them. Vainly it attempted to take the *Boston* in tow. Later an American destroyer pulled alongside and took the flyers aboard, while a line was fastened from the destroyer's boom to the plane to haul it up onto the deck. When the plane was suspended in midair halfway up, the boom broke. The *Boston* smashed into the ocean and vanished.

That left two planes, half the original expedition.

The *New Orleans* and the *Chicago* made the final long over-water jumps safely to North America. The *Boston*'s dejected crew

Billy Mitchell

came to Nova Scotia by ship, where they became airborne again in a spare World Cruiser flown up from the United States and christened *Boston II*. Reaching the U.S. at last, the six aviators made a triumphal tour across the country, including a call on President Calvin Coolidge at the White House. When they landed at Los Angeles, the crowd was so enthusiastic in trying to reach the planes that it knocked the flyers down while grabbing for souvenirs. Lieutenant Smith was startled because one woman cut a piece out of his collar with scissors and another welcomer snipped out a bit from the seat of his pants. Flying in an Arctic snowstorm was almost safer!

Finally, Seattle! To the very last moment, the flight was a team effort. In order that no one could claim to be the first man to fly around the world, the three planes flew across the Seattle landing field wingtip-to-wingtip, sharing equally in the glory.

The trip around the world had been slow, perilous, and delayed by obstacles as unpredictable as those faced by Magellan's sailors. From the time Magellan's ship completed man's first circumnavigation of the earth, until the World Cruisers landed in Seattle, 402 years had passed. Nobody, not even the imaginative Jules Verne had he still been alive, would have dared to forecast that in just another thirty-eight years American astronauts would be hurtling around the earth in space capsules more than a hundred miles up. Instead of the 175 days the first world flight required, the Mercury astronauts completed each trip around our planet in less than one and a half hours. From that height they saw the earth as a giant globe hanging in space in a way that was impossible for the men in the low-flying World Cruisers. And only seven years after the first satellite flight, American airmen stretched man's skill another, almost unbelievable, giant leap forward by landing on the moon.

— 5 —

The Mail Must Go Through

Half a century ago, most civilian flying was done by barnstorming and stunt pilots. Few planes had room for passengers, except singly in the second open cockpit. Many Americans were afraid to fly, anyway. They wouldn't have gone up in an airplane if they had the opportunity.

This fear isn't surprising when we remember how risky airplanes were. Newspapers published more stories about planes that crashed, killing their pilots, than they did about aerial achievements such as the around-the-world flight. Airplanes still were regarded widely as dangerous toys. Few of them had room for passengers.

A few civilians were more adventurous, like an elderly aunt of this writer. Having learned of a plane that made the trip with a few passengers, she announced to her surprised relatives that she was going to fly from a Chicago visit back to her home in Indiana. They protested her foolhardiness.

She retorted, "I'm so old it doesn't matter much if I do get killed. And I want to see what it's like to fly before I die." Aunt Lote not only arrived safely but lived quite a few more years, during which she taunted her younger relatives about an old woman's being the first in the family to fly.

When airplanes began to carry the mail, they found a practical use for the first time outside war. Letters taken by plane arrived sooner than those carried by train—most of the time—and hurried

U.S. stamp commemorates 50th anniversary of Air Mail Service.

up the pace of business between cities. From the pioneer airmail routes developed in the United States during the 1920's sprang the giant airlines of today. Jetliners now streak through the skies with long white vapor trails in their wake carrying thousands of pounds of mail, along with their passengers.

It wasn't that way at first. For a decade the mail mostly was flown in two-cockpit open biplanes like those used by the barnstormers. Even the faithful, plodding old Jenny turned up on some mail routes. Mail sacks were stacked in one cockpit, and on heavy days additional sacks were stuffed into the pilot's cockpit, leaving just enough space for him to move his legs. At the height of the Christmas rush on a route in the Northwest, pilots even tied overflow mail sacks onto the struts that held the wings together. They took off with a prayer that the additional wind resistance thus created wouldn't prevent the plane from getting into the air. Aircraft designers calculating stresses and lifting capabilities of a plane never visualized that kind of extra load on the wings. But they didn't know the early airmail pilots, a breed of flyers who mixed the risk-taking of the stunt pilots with a dedication to the Post Office's demand that the mail must get through. The Post Office adopted its motto, "Neither snow, nor rain, nor heat, nor gloom of night stays these couriers from the swift completion of their appointed rounds," years before the first airmail flight, but it describes well the attitude of the mail-plane pilots. Many of them were killed. Others escaped alive only by jumping from disabled planes at night into unmarked darkness and praying that their parachutes would open. Frequently in the first years, sacks of mail that started from a city by air reached their destination by train, after being removed from a grounded or wrecked plane.

At first, United States Army pilots flew the mail. The Aerial Mail Service began during 1918, a few months before World War I ended. The United States had become air-conscious because hundreds of its young men were being trained for flight service with the American Expeditionary Force in France, and some of them were in combat against German pilots. Dim inklings of the airplane's potential were becoming apparent.

In the beginning, the only airmail route ran between New York and Washington. The planes landed at Philadelphia, so the mail sacks could be tossed into fresh planes, much as letters once were carried in relays across the West by the Pony Express. It was impossible for a Jenny to go nonstop the entire 218-mile route from the field in New Jersey that served as New York City's terminal to the polo field alongside the Potomac River in Washington which was the national capital's primitive airfield.

President Woodrow Wilson drove over from the White House on the morning of May 15 to watch the first airmail plane depart from Washington. He waited for the takeoff, and waited some more. The Army officers in charge grew increasingly disturbed and the President increasingly impatient. The plane's engine wouldn't start. When the pilot shouted, "Contact!" a soldier gave the wooden propellor a whirl. Nothing happened. Another try, then another. The stubborn propellor wouldn't go around.

The first airmail plane takes off from Washington, D.C., for Philadelphia while President Woodrow Wilson watches. The pilot became lost and crashed in Virginia.

"That's strange. It flew fine yesterday," the pilot said.

This was many years before airplanes had self-starters. Turning a propellor by hand was risky for anyone not agile and alert. If the engine caught and the propellor whirled, the man on the ground had to jump back quickly to escape its blades. Sometimes two or three men joined hands in a human chain to give the propellor extra turnover power. Even that couldn't get the Jenny to run on this historic ceremonial morning. In the presence of the President, she behaved like a stubborn little girl asked to perform on the piano for company.

At last, an Army officer had an idea. "Check the gasoline tank!" he commanded.

It was bone dry. No wonder the Jenny wouldn't behave!

For safety purposes, someone had drained the gasoline the previous night. In the excitement the next morning, nobody had remembered to fill the tank.

With a wave to President Wilson, the pilot belatedly took off for Philadelphia with his cargo of first-day mail—in the wrong direction.

How it happened, nobody was certain. Instead of turning north on the 128-mile flight to Philadelphia, he became confused and headed south. When the Jenny failed to reach Philadelphia to connect with the waiting relay plane to New York, a search was begun. Eventually the pilot turned up twenty miles southeast of Washington. Realizing that he was lost, he had tried to land the Jenny on a country road and ask a farmer for directions. He smashed up the plane. The mail sack had to be taken by truck and put aboard a train to Philadelphia.

Mostly what the Aerial Mail Service received from its first day of operation was embarrassment, an inglorious start for a service that was to record remarkable stories of reliability and heroism. The southbound airmail sack from New York did reach Washington on schedule, fortunately.

Postal patrons had little reason to use the service in its early period, beyond the novelty of having a letter stamped "Air Mail," and few did. The regular mail by train was delivered to its recipients at the same time as the aerial letters, for two cents an

U.S. stamp commemorates 200 years of postal service.

ounce instead of sixteen. Not until longer routes were started, such as New York to Chicago, did the potential of the airplane for saving time begin to be apparent.

After three months, the job of flying the mail was turned over to civilian pilots employed by the Post Office. Most of them were given a different kind of plane, the DH-4. That was the official designation for these two-cockpit open biplanes; the pilots called them "Flaming Coffins."

Grim truth lay behind that picturesque nickname. The DH-4's engine in the nose of the plane had short exhaust pipes. In flight these became so hot that they glowed, right in the face of the pilot, who sat in the front cockpit, behind the engine and the gasoline tank. Mail was stored in the other cockpit behind him. When a pilot made a crash landing or when the undercarriage collapsed as the wheels touched the ground, as often happened, the plane dug its nose into the earth, frequently crushing the pilot between the engine and the mail load. The job was so dangerous that of the first forty pilots hired by the Post Office Department in 1918, thirty-one had died in crashes by 1925.

The airmail pilot in his coveralls, helmet and goggles, and carrying a .45 caliber revolver to protect the mail, was a romantic figure to the public. He didn't have much success in buying life insurance, however. Under the kind of federal rules existing today, none of those early airmail planes would be allowed to leave the ground. The route from New York to Cleveland was considered especially perilous, because it passed over mountains that frequently were shrouded in cloud and fog.

Eventually, the DH-4 planes were modified. The pilot was placed in the rear, the mail in front, and longer exhaust pipes were installed to remove that dangerous glare from the pilot's vision.

As the airmail service grew to serve more cities, night flights became necessary for the first time. Pilots needed to leave a city in early evening, after the close of the business day, and arrive in the destination city before morning, so the airmail letters could be delivered the day after they were posted. Otherwise, the mail might as well go by train.

It was these night flights that caused so many crashes. The pilots had weather reports they couldn't trust, compasses that frequently spun crazily, no radios, and of course no radar. Ice forming on the wings, weighing down the plane and freezing the controls, was a constant peril, much feared. Another critical lack was an instrument to show whether the plane was flying level, climbing, or falling. When a pilot in a black mass of fog maneuvered to find a hole in it, he easily became confused. Clammy moisture filled the cockpit and smothered visibility. He might be diving toward the ground or flying almost upside down without knowing it.

Some pilots fastened a carpenter's level in the cockpit, hoping that the bubble in the level would show whether the plane was on an even keel. One pilot taped a partially emptied half pint of whisky to the instrument panel, using the top of the liquid contents as a level. If it didn't work and he crashed, he said, he could drink the rest of the bottle as a stimulant to help him survive until help came.

No lighted runways welcomed the mail flyers at the end of their runs. The fields generally were raw dirt and grass, bumpy and small, often with trees or other obstacles at the end of the short runways. When the ground crew at a landing field heard the engine drone of a plane circling in the clouds, trying to find the field, they sometimes turned on a searchlight and beamed it into the sky, or burned gasoline at the end of the runway. Even this skimpy aid wasn't enough on stormy nights. Eventually, beacon lights at intervals of several miles were installed in a line

ABOVE: *Loading sacks into mail compartment under armed guard, 1927.* BELOW: *Mail today is placed on jetliners in containers which are rolled into the plane.*

along the mail plane routes; these were a great help except on nights so dense that they could not be seen from the air.

Yet the pilots were expected to take off on their mail flights night after night, no matter what the weather, and somehow or another get those precious mail sacks to the scheduled destinations on time. Often enough, they knew that only instinct and luck would get them through. The admirable thing is how frequently they accomplished their mission.

One of those airmail pilots, flying the night mail between Chicago and St. Louis, was Charles Augustus Lindbergh. That name would be praised around the world later on, but he was unknown then, just another young ex-barnstormer fortunate enough to get an airmail job. On a miserable night as he approached Chicago from St. Louis, Lindbergh flew into a bank of impenetrable fog. His first thought was to make a forced landing in some farmer's field, using his single flare to illuminate the ground. But the release mechanism for the flare failed to function.

Lindbergh's next alternative was to climb above the fog, continue to Checkerboard Field, the airmail field a few miles west of Chicago at Maywood, and hope he could see enough to land. He found the general area, recognizing it by the diffused glow of city lights through the overcast, but no gap in the fog. For half an hour he circled above the field, in such heavy weather that he could not see the drums of gasoline the worried ground crew burned as a beacon.

His own gasoline was running low. He did not want to crash in a built-up urban area, so he swung around southwest again into the country. Soon his engine sputtered and died, the main gasoline tank dry. Cutting on the small reserve tank, he knew that he had only twenty minutes of flying time left. Mile after mile, the fog stretched on. Lindbergh realized he could not escape it with the few pints of fuel remaining. Either he must crash blindly in the plane, or he must jump by parachute into the black unknown.

Risky as it was, the parachute jump was the safer course. Accordingly, Lindbergh climbed to an altitude of five thousand feet, put his flashlight in the pocket of his flying suit, and when the

Charles Augustus Lindbergh

engine coughed its last stepped out over the side of the cockpit.
After counting to three, the traditional time a jumper used to
make certain that he was clear of the abandoned plane, he pulled
the ripcord. A welcome jerk tugged his shoulders as the chute
opened.

Drifting down, he beamed the flashlight onto the top of the fog
bank in the hope of seeing through it. Nothing! Startled, he heard
the sound of an airplane heading toward him. Would that unexpected plane fly straight into his parachute and rip it to bits?

Soon the truth became apparent: the plane was his own. Since
it appeared to be out of gas when he jumped, he foolishly hadn't
bothered to turn off the engine switch. As the pilotless plane's
nose dropped, enough gasoline drained into the carburetor to give

the engine a little more life. The runaway plane was circling around Lindbergh, no more than a hundred yards at times, as man and plane fell at approximately the same speed. Five times the plane circled the parachutist; then it disappeared.

As Lindbergh tugged on the ropes of the parachute to maneuver away from the plane, he dropped his flashlight. This left him no way to see the ground toward which he was falling. All he could do was hold his feet together, pull up his knees, put his hands over his face and hope that he would strike soft, open dirt.

Luckily, he did. He sprawled in a field of tall corn, jarred but uninjured. Gathering up his parachute, he tucked the folds under his arm and walked between rows of corn until he found a dirt road. When an automobile's headlights approached, he flagged it down and obtained a ride to the nearest farm house. The rural party line telephone buzzed with neighbors chattering about the wreck. One of them reported that the plane had crashed about two miles away, after just missing a house. Lindbergh went to the wreckage, gathered up the mailbags, and carried them to the nearest post office to be sent ahead by train. The airmail got

A Swallow biplane, which carried airmail when private companies took over the service in 1926, sits beside a current-day medium-size United Airlines jetliner.

First coast-to-coast air travelers in 1927 flew between San Francisco and Chicago in this Boeing 40A plane, which had space for two passengers in addition to the mail.

through, even if it did arrive in Chicago many hours late aboard a railroad mail car.

That jump made Lindbergh a member of the Caterpillar Club. Qualifying for Caterpillar membership was easy. All you had to do was to make an emergency parachute jump and survive to tell about it. For that, the fortunate pilot received a gold pin from a parachute manufacturer. Lindbergh became a four-time member of the informal organization, having to make that many leaps for his life. Other airmail pilots gained membership, too, under similar circumstances. Parachuting then was not the sport it is now. The only persons who "hit the silk" were demonstration jumpers at air shows, under well controlled conditions, and pilots saving their lives.

After flying the mail for eight years with its own pilots, of whom it had about a hundred at one time, the Post Office turned over the task to private companies. Each mail route was offered to the firm making the highest bid. The winners became known as contract air carriers. They promised to fly the mail over the designated route on agreed-upon schedules; the Post Office paid them per pound of mail flown. Most of the routes were organized to

97

branch out from the fundamental transcontinental route: New York–Chicago–Salt Lake City–San Francisco. The Chicago–St. Louis and Salt Lake City–Los Angeles routes were examples of the "feeder" arrangement.

Service on these Civil Air Mail routes began early in 1926, although Post Office pilots continued to operate the main transcontinental route for another year. By that time, after nine years of flying the mail, the Post Office had lost forty-three pilots killed, while twenty-three had been seriously injured.

The companies which won the airmail contracts were beginners in the business of organized flying. Each had a few pilots, old planes, and little money. Their income was derived almost entirely from the fees the Post Office paid them for the weight of mail they transported. Some companies, when their cash was low, hid bricks in the bottoms of mailbags, under the airmail letters, so they could collect larger fees from the government.

That is how today's giant airlines were born. These pioneer contract mail carriers of a half century ago began commercial aviation in the United States. United Airlines, Western Airlines, and Trans World Airlines, to name just three, trace their origin directly to small companies that got started when they won Civil Air Mail contracts.

Carrying the mail was all that most of these contract carrier companies did at first. Mostly, they used planes with the traditional open cockpits. If the mail load was light, as it often was, they occasionally bundled up an adventurous passenger in flying suit and goggles and carried him or her for a fee, tucked in among the mail sacks.

In good weather, with their planes performing properly, the airmail pilots found their long, slow trips dull. Alone in the cockpit, the pilot had no one to talk with and no radio for conversation with the ground. So he was glad to have company, even though they could communicate only by shouting or passing notes. Lindbergh spent part of his hours aloft calculating how he might fly the Atlantic. Pilots in the Southwest dipped low to shoot at coyotes with their .45's. Another trick they played on night flights across the desert was to fly head-on at an approaching train with their

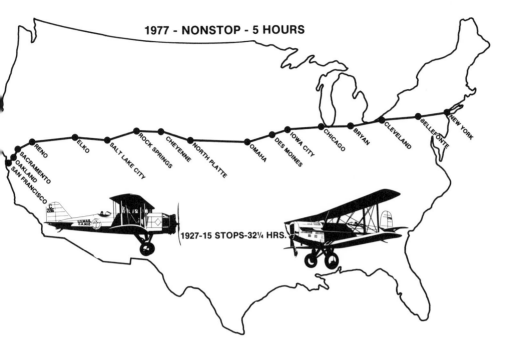

1927-15 STOPS-32¼ HRS.

When coast-to-coast service was inaugurated in 1927, it involved 17 cities and 15 intermediate stops. Today jetliners cross the continent in five hours nonstop.

lights on, then at the last moment turn off the lights and zoom up over the top of the locomotive, upsetting the engineer. Such stunts were forbidden, but the pilots did them, anyway. Nobody was around to catch them.

Pilots of the Varney company, which operated a mail route through mountainous country in the Northwest, were a happy-go-lucky lot. One landed once with a black eye. He had detoured for some aerial sight-seeing up a canyon at low level, and a pheasant flew between the wings of his biplane, hitting him in the face! Varney's planes had no extra oomph under the best of circumstances, and with a heavy load of mail they could not get through a certain high mountain pass under bad weather conditions. The ingenious pilots solved that problem: they landed their planes on a straight stretch of mountain road near the summit. Here they waited until a passing wagon came along to tow them over the crest; then they took off again on the down slope. That is why Varney pilots carried ropes in their flying equipment.

Much as railroad engineers came to know the residents along their routes, the early airmail flyers developed a personal feeling for families living on farms along their routes and waved to them as they passed. The pilots of a Western Air Express route learned about the death of one farmer who had faithfully turned on a light each night at an emergency landing field. His widow was left with eight children. To the surprise of the family, on Christmas the daily mail plane flew low over their farm and dropped gifts for the children and an envelope of money for the mother. The pilot circled and tilted the plane so the mother and children could see what he was wearing, a Santa Claus suit over his flight coveralls.

Gradually, the mail lines obtained planes that could carry a few passengers, two or three persons at first, and later aircraft capable of carrying ten passengers. By the standards of the early 1930's, these were comparable to the huge Boeing 747's of today. Several lines used the all-metal Ford trimotored plane nicknamed the "Tin Goose," a dependable workhorse which had an engine in the nose and one suspended under each wing.

Records of the Post Office are filled with stories about heroism and helpfulness by pilots of mail planes. A pilot flying from Chicago to Atlanta looked down to see a house on fire at Centralia,

The Ford trimotor plane known affectionately as the "Tin Goose" carried airmail and passengers slowly but steadily when the commercial airlines were growing up during the 1930's.

In the early 1930's this was one of the largest passenger planes flying. A U.S. Mail emblem appears just in front of the wing.

Illinois. He flew low, "zoomed" his motor, and wakened the occupants, who ran outside just before the roof collapsed. Another pilot in the West hit a mountain at the 7,800-foot level but fortunately fell into a snowbank twelve feet deep. After hours of waiting, he was reached by rescuers. Together they rolled the mail sacks down the mountain and put them on packhorses, which carried them to a nearby airport. There the pilot loaded them aboard another plane and flew it to Salt Lake City, his original destination. The mail did get through.

One of the most amazing stories involves a trimotored plane. Pilot Mal R. Freeburg was flying it from St. Paul, Minnesota, to Chicago with a heavy load of mail and eight passengers. At an altitude of two thousand feet, he felt a severe vibration in the left motor. Part of the propellor fell off. Moments later the motor ripped out of its mounting and lodged on the left landing-gear struts.

The situation was critical. The engine hanging near the wheels upset the balance of the plane. Fighting hard to keep the craft level with his remaining two engines, Freeburg flew it over the middle of the Mississippi River. There he went into a series of turns, dips, and climbs that further upset the frightened passengers. These gyrations succeeded in their purpose, however. They shook the motor loose from its lodging place, and with a final tilt of the plane, Freeburg dumped it splashing into the river far below. Then he brought his passengers and mail to a safe landing.

After the private companies had been flying the mail for nearly eight years, the federal government suspected that some of the contracts had been obtained illegally. On short notice, President Franklin D. Roosevelt canceled all private mail contracts and announced that the United States Army Air Corps would take over the job of flying the mail.

"You have ten days in which to organize the mail service and start it flying," Major General Benjamin B. Foulois was told.

Hardly anyone realized what an unfair assignment was being handed to the poorly prepared and equipped military pilots. They had not been trained for night mail-carrying work, they had old planes, and they were unacquainted with the routes. The commander-in-chief said to obey orders and fly the mail, anyway. They did.

The result was tragic. During the first six weeks of Air Corps mail flying, twelve pilots were killed and fifteen injured critically. The series of sad newspaper headlines angered the public; Washington was besieged with demands to do something. After three and a half months, new contracts were written and the task of carrying the mail was returned to private companies. They have had it ever since. Instead of being a luxury service used mostly by business firms that needed fast communication over long distance, the airmail today carries eighty per cent of all first class letters between cities. This is done automatically at regular postage rates, without the use of air mail stamps being necessary.

General Foulois claimed later that despite its fatal crashes, the period when the Air Corps pilots flew the mail had an extremely valuable result. A tight-fisted Congress, seeing how ill-prepared the peacetime Air Corps was, was jarred into making fresh money available for better planes and pilot training, so that when the United States was drawn into World War II seven years later, its air force was far better prepared than it would have been without such shock treatment.

102

6

Dinosaurs of the Sky

A majestic and fascinating sight appeared to a cluster of people waiting on a hillside in northern Illinois one bright afternoon in the mid-1920's. Among them was this writer, then a boy. Into our vision from the right floated a long slim silvery balloon, like an enormous cigar drifting across the sky. Here was grandeur. It was by far the biggest thing we had ever seen in the sky, making the single-motored biplanes of those days seem like toys. At a leisurely speed this canvas-covered ship of the heavens glided across the horizon about a thousand feet above the ground. Sunshine reflected from its curved sides; a moving shadow struck the earth below it.

Bold letters on the side of the airship said U.S. NAVY, and near the finned tail behind the red, white, and blue star emblem was the name, *Shenandoah*. This was the first dirigible built in the United States, indeed one of a relative handful of these massive rigid balloons ever built anywhere.

To those of us watching below, the *Shenandoah* seemed to move in serene dignity. We didn't realize how tricky it was for the dirigible's crew to control her in flight and what a delicate balancing act the captain had been doing to fly the behemoth on an even keel since he had given the command, "Up ship!" at takeoff.

When he gave the order, the ground crew released ropes restraining the dirigible, and it rose straight up silently to a pre-

103

This pioneer dirigible, photographed near Los Angeles in 1910, was a forerunner of the airships that later carried scores of passengers and crewmen across the Atlantic Ocean in comfort. The pilot flew the balloon from a walkway suspended underneath the gas bag.

calculated height of a few hundred feet. This was done by the buoyancy of the helium gas contained in twenty large bags housed inside the outer envelope of aluminum-painted canvas. Each bag was lined with the stomach linings of oxen to prevent leaks. Once airborne, the dirigible was propelled forward by its set of engines slung beneath its frame. The captain presided in a command gondola, much like the bridge of a ship; this too hung beneath the great canvas bag.

Flying a dirigible was quite different from flying an airplane, and few Americans were trained in the craft during the few years after World War I during which the mammoth balloons appeared in American skies.

If the captain desired to take the *Shenandoah* to a higher altitude in flight—to avoid a thunderstorm, for example—he could not point its nose sharply upward, as an airplane pilot does. The airship was so big and its air speed so slow, relatively, that too sharp an ascent angle made it stall and drop its tail dangerously.

Hundreds of gallons of water were stowed aboard in tanks. In order to gain altitude, the dirigible must be made lighter. At the command "Discharge ballast!" valves were opened and water cascaded from the bottom of the airship. This made the *Shenandoah* lighter, and it rose.

104

When the commander desired a lower altitude, he ordered, "Vent gas!" Crewmen pulled toggle switches in the control car and designated amounts of helium were released from the bags. This removed some of the buoyancy, making the dirigible heavier, and it dropped softly to a lower altitude. If the commander wished to point the *Shenandoah*'s nose lower, in preparation for landing, he "trimmed" the ship by having gas released only from the forward bags. As the gasoline supply was consumed by the engines on long trips, the airship rose because its weight was reduced; this extra buoyancy had to be offset by venting more gas. Thus, keeping the dirigible on an even keel at a desired altitude was a constant problem in applied physics and mathematics.

This control work was relatively simple for experienced crewmen in calm weather, such as the day on which we watched. When the giant craft was whipped around by bad weather, however, the utmost skill was required to hold it steady. We awed spectators didn't realize it, but the *Shenandoah* was headed for disaster in just such circumstances, one in a series of spectacular wrecks that doomed early aviation's attempt to make the dirigible the rival of the airplane. Indeed, if the boosters of dirigibles had been correct, travelers would be crossing the oceans in gigantic airships today instead of jet airplanes.

Time and tragedy proved them wrong. They didn't want to admit how unreliable the big gas-bag containers were, and they couldn't foresee how fast and spacious passenger airplanes would become. So the dirigibles vanished from the sky eventually. But in the twenty years these airborne mammoths roamed the world, they thrilled millions of earthbound spectators and provided memorable trips for the few thousand well-to-do persons who could afford to ride on them across oceans and between continents.

An airplane flies because an engine, or more than one, drives it forward fast enough for the lifting surfaces of its wings to carry the heavier-than-air machine away from the earth. A simple balloon goes aloft because its bag is filled with hot air, which rises through the atmosphere, or with a gas that is lighter than

In this one-man dirigible balloon, A. Roy Knabenshue made the first airship flight over Manhattan. Here he is seen taking off from the west side of Central Park in New York City, at Sixty-second Street, for a flight to Forty-second Street and back.

Visitors to the St. Louis Fair were excited by flights of this primitive dirigible, the California Arrow. Like other pioneer airships, it had a gas bag of Japanese silk filled with hydrogen. The frame on which the pilot stood was wooden.

Two views of construction on airship with a rigid frame, introduced at the turn of the century. LEFT: *The aluminum framework.* RIGHT: *Final protective cover of ramie fiber.*

air. The principle is that if a balloon is to fly, the total weight of the gas, bag, frame, and load of the balloon must be less than the air which would occupy the same space.

A gas balloon shaped horizontally and given an engine for power becomes an airship. If the bag can be filled completely with gas, and collapses when empty, it is a blimp. A few blimps still are in operation, such as the ones we see circling football stadiums flashing advertising messages.

The ultimate development of the balloon was the huge dirigible, an airship with a rigid frame of lightweight aluminum alloy over which a canvas cover was stretched. Inside the frame, the lifting gas was contained in a series of large bags harnessed to the metal structure, leaving space within the "envelope" for walkways, living quarters, freight storage, and other service facilities.

Although a dirigible when loaded weighed two hundred tons or more, it was called a lighter-than-air craft because its lifting power was provided by its gas.

As described earlier, men first rose into the air aboard a hot air balloon in 1783. Thus the balloon had a head start of 120 years over the airplane. Hydrogen, a very light gas, soon replaced hot air as the lifting power of these free-floating balloons.

Balloon ascensions were popular long before the airplane was invented. This poster advertised one in England in 1837.

Balloon ascensions were entertainment during the 1800's.

Once in France a duel was fought in balloons by two men who argued over the love of a woman. Instead of pacing off the required distance, turning, and firing at each other in the traditional style of dueling, they took to the sky. When the balloons were several hundred feet in the air, and about eighty yards

Count Zeppelin's airship in the boat shed. LEFT: *The framework, the covering, the bridge, a car, and one of the air screws.* ABOVE: *The airship ready for the ascent.*

apart, the signal to fire was given. One man's shot hit the bag of his foe's balloon; the gas bag crashed to the ground, killing both the rival dueler and his second.

Gas bags tethered to the ground were used as observation posts by the Northern forces in the Civil War. Only when a wealthy German army officer, Count Ferdinand von Zeppelin, conceived the idea of a balloon with a rigid frame in the 1890's did the thought of using an airship for travel between points become practical.

Zeppelin took his first dirigible aloft over Lake Constance in southern Germany in July, 1900, more than three years before the Wright brothers made their historic heavier-than-air flight. The count was so much the "father" of dirigibles that they became known generally not as airships but as "Zeppelins." One of the most famous of them was named the *Graf Zeppelin* (Graf means count in German).

Zeppelin's original dirigible was 420 feet long, about half the

On July 2, 1900, Count Zeppelin's airship rose smoothly and quietly above Lake Constance.

The airship pictured some 1300 feet above the surface of the lake.

The airship landing. The cars dipped only two inches into the water.

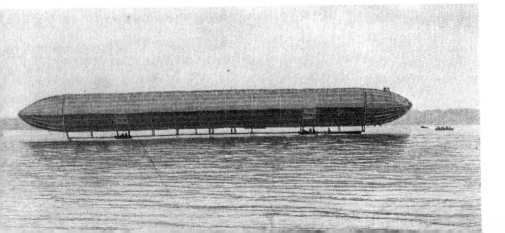

Two dirigibles at the Dominguez Air Show near Los Angeles in 1910 were piloted by Lincoln Beachey and Roy Knabenshue. In a race, Beachey, above, was beaten by an airplane piloted by Louis Paulhan.

size of later models, and had seventeen gas bags inside the shell. Instead of containing crew facilities inside the frame, this first dirigible had a gallery 346 feet long suspended under the bag. At two points along this external walkway were control stations for the crew. The upward-downward pointing of the dirigible's nose was controlled in a primitive manner: a cable was suspended the length of the airship, along which a weight could be pulled. When the weight was drawn toward the stern, the dirigible's nose went up; when it was pulled forward, the nose dipped.

Simple and slow as these first motor-driven airships were, they traveled more rapidly than the earliest airplanes. When airship was pitted against airplane at Dominguez Field near Los Angeles at America's first really big air show in 1910, it was for close to the last time. The narrow speed margin was erased forever as airplanes were improved.

The Zeppelins, growing in size, became deadly military weapons during World War I, from 1914 to 1918, when they flew over London at night and dropped bombs on the British capital. Although they did little damage compared to the German

When this balloon circled the Capitol in June, 1906, business in Congress was suspended while senators and representatives gathered outside to watch.

bomber raids on London during World War II, and several of them were shot down, they created terror and hatred. Thus, when World War I ended, the victorious Allies placed severe limitations on what the defeated Germans could do with their postwar airships. The victors, especially Great Britain and the United States, decided to use Zeppelin's ideas and build airships of their own. This led to what might be called the Age of the Zeppelin, the period until the dirigibles passed from the scene.

Years before Lindbergh won renown for his New York–to–Paris flight, men flew across the Atlantic in a dirigible. Aboard the British R-34 in 1919 were thirty adventurous men including an American, Lieutenant Commander Zachary Lansdowne of the United States Navy, riding as an observer. The R-34 was put aloft in Scotland in midsummer and sailed westward at an altitude of fifteen hundred feet above the ocean, landing safely on Long Island. This could hardly be called a demonstration of speed since it required 108 hours, or nearly five days. The fastest ships could make the crossing almost as quickly.

The first and strangest attempt to cross the Atlantic in an airship took place long before that, in 1910.

A hydrogen-filled gas bag named the *America*, with two engines of only eighty horsepower each, tried to fly from Atlantic City, New Jersey, to somewhere in Europe, anywhere it happened to reach. A journalist named Walter Wellman, having twice failed to reach the North Pole in his airship, had decided upon the transatlantic flight instead. The *America* was a strange craft, even for a day when inventors had weird notions of what would fly. Beneath the gas bag a flimsy canvas-walled control car was suspended, and under it a lifeboat. Strangest of all was a 300-foot-long snakelike device Wellman called an equilibrator. This was a steel cable hanging down from the airship on which were strung thirty small tanks full of gasoline, like beads on a string, and at the end, forty wooden blocks. The device was flexible and designed to float.

In the air, the *America* looked like a sausage with a long tail. The equilibrator was supposed to hold the *America* about two hundred feet above the ocean at all times, so that the crew would not have to release hydrogen or water ballast as the varying temperatures of daylight and darkness changed the airship's buoyancy.

Wellman and a crew of five took off from Atlantic City on October 15, 1910, to the cheers of holiday-makers on the boardwalk. That was a Saturday morning. Soon everything went wrong. The two motors failed. Far from helping, the equilibrator was a hindrance. The *America* was buffeted by winds aimlessly for three days, until early Tuesday the crew climbed down into the lifeboat and the airship sank slowly into the Atlantic waves. They were rescued by a passing ship about four hundred miles out from the American coast, after having zigzagged at the whims of the winds for over a thousand miles. Even though it failed, it was by far the longest trip in the air by a powered vehicle up to that time. Wellman was so disappointed that he never flew again. As for the equilibrator, it vanished into the never-never land of inventors' bad dreams.

Seeing the Atlantic crossed by the R-34 excited the Americans, who wanted a dirigible of their own. So they built one. Working from captured German plans, the Navy constructed the *Shenan-*

Walter Wellman's balloon America *about to make a forced landing in the sea after its transatlantic attempt failed. The picture was taken from the rescue ship* Trent.

doah, a name which in some Indian languages means "daughter of the stars."

For two years after the *Shenandoah* first went aloft in September, 1923, the airship toured the United States, gave rides to prominent persons, functioned as scouting "eyes" for the Navy in maneuvers and impressed observers by mooring at sea to a mast built at the stern of a converted fuel tanker. Commander Lansdowne became her captain and a rather romantic figure to his fellow Americans.

One advantage of dirigibles over airplanes was their ability to fly long distances without landing, even right through the night, which airplane pilots usually didn't do then. At night, navigating the *Shenandoah* was less than certain, and the crew weren't always sure exactly where they were.

On a trip to the West Coast, night found the *Shenandoah* over southeastern Arizona. The navigators were uncertain whether the town below was Bisbee or Douglas. By radio, the airship's commander asked a radio station in the town for help. He messaged, "We can see the headlights of cars on streets in town. Please ask the motorists to help us by blinking their lights. If they see us over Douglas, blink them quickly. If this is Bisbee, blink them slowly."

Soon the officers looking below saw motorists blinking their headlights slowly. It was Bisbee. Huge as the dirigible was, its crewmen, like the barnstorming airplane pilots, did their share of flying by the seat of their pants!

In 1924 the Navy acquired a second, even larger dirigible, the *Los Angeles,* built by the defeated Germans as part of the payment to the United States for losing World War I. Optimistic plans for use of giant airships were discussed, including flights over the North and South poles.

Then, just one day before the *Shenandoah's* second birthday, disaster came.

The ship had sailed west from her base at Lakehurst, New Jersey, to tour Midwestern state fairs. Early on the morning of September 4, 1925, in the blackness before sunup, the *Shenandoah* flew into a thunderstorm over Ohio, the kind of weather

A biplane flying alongside the Shenandoah *above Los Angeles in 1924 shows the huge difference in size between the dirigible and the airplanes of that period.*

dirigible commanders tried to avoid. Lightning streaks stabbed the sky, illuminating the silver giant. The headwind was so strong that the *Shenandoah* almost stood still; her motors could not push her bulk forward against the force of nature.

Almost battling clear of the thunderstorm, the airship developed engine trouble and, buffeted by high winds, began rising. Lansdowne and his crew used all the tricks they knew, but despite the effort of the helmsman to get her nose pointed down, the airship lifted to an altitude of six thousand feet, far above her normal course. The storm twisted her into a spinning motion.

In the control car, the crew felt a shivering lurch. "The ship is gone!" one man exclaimed.

Moments later, tossing and rolling at weird angles, out of control, the *Shenandoah* broke in two, about a third of the way back from the nose. Crewmen inside the airship at the point of the break were thrown into open air. Some grabbed dangling struts and torn wires to avoid falling through space.

The back section, longer and heavier, plummeted into the earth, open end first, tail sticking into the air. As it hit the ground, the massive structure crumbled into a jumble of framework, bracing wires, smashed engines, and canvas. Inside it several men were trapped. Others were thrown free, either to survive or die at the whim of luck.

That left the smaller front section drifting aloft as a free balloon, its rear open to the elements. Having no controls, it was tossed around by the twisting winds, but it had enough gas bags intact to remain buoyant. It rose to eight thousand feet and then started down again. For nearly an hour it tossed around helplessly, carrying those crewmen who had been up forward when the airship split apart. Then it nosed into a hillside cornfield, missed a house, ripped through trees, and came to rest.

When the victims were pulled from the debris and the surviving Navy men mustered for a roll call, the count showed fourteen crewmen dead and twenty-nine miraculously still alive.

Despite this tragedy, the Navy still believed in dirigibles. It ordered an even larger one built, and named it the *Akron* for the Ohio city where it was constructed. Lessons learned from the *Shenandoah* were applied in building the new airship.

The *Akron* was so large that it actually swallowed airplanes into its belly. Hangar space for naval scout planes was provided inside the envelope, which served as a mother ship somewhat as an aircraft carrier does. A triangular catching apparatus was suspended under the *Akron*. As one of her planes returned from a scouting mission, the pilot flew it close under the airship at the slowest speed possible, not much faster than the *Akron* was traveling. A hook attached to the plane's wing caught the triangular apparatus. Once snared in this manner, the airplane was pulled up inside the airship. It could take off from this midair platform by being lowered below the airship, revving up its motor, and disconnecting the hook. The planes never were aboard the *Akron* when she left the ground, however, because their weight hindered her takeoff. They flew up later for a midair rendezvous.

The *Akron* was involved in a weird and frightening episode in May, 1932, while attempting a landing at Camp Kearney, near San Diego, California. Landing a dirigible was complicated business, involving a ground crew of two hundred men. Their job in part was to seize two long ropes dropped from the airship and hold her steady while a steel cable that had been tossed from the craft's nose opening to the mooring mast was drawn taut mechanically.

This particular crew was inexperienced. As they dug in their heels and tugged at the ropes, the mechanical apparatus winding in the steel cable broke. It began unwinding. Suddenly, the *Akron* had pulled free from the mooring mast and was rising skyward.

All the ground crewmen let go of the ropes except three who, caught by surprise, found themselves dangling in the air as the *Akron* rose higher. One lost his grip and fell to earth. So did the second man. Both were killed. That left eighteen-year-old apprentice seaman "Bud" Cowart hanging desperately by a hand grip on the big rope as the *Akron* rose to fifteen hundred feet. Heavy winds made impossible the idea of easing the dirigible close enough to the ground for him to drop off safely. To be saved, he would have to hang on while the rope was pulled up into the *Akron.*

In the nose of the dirigible, the crew rigged the rope over the drum of a small winch. Foot by foot, as the seaman swung in the wind like a pendulum, they wound the rope up through the hatch. Cowart hung on. His white seaman's cap started to blow off; he took one hand off the rope long enough to shove the cap inside his uniform shirt.

After half an hour of clinging to his lifeline, he called up to the hatch, "Hey, when are you going to land?"

"Hang on!" an officer shouted. "We'll get you in soon."

Thirty minutes later, Cowart was winched up to the open gangway and pulled aboard. The first thing he asked for was a tour of the airship!

Fate in the end was no kinder to the *Akron* than it had been to the *Shenandoah.* After only eighteen months of operation, it too crashed in a storm, off the Atlantic coast. This time the death list was worse; only three of the seventy-six men aboard survived. That was on April 3, 1933.

Roy Knabenshue, who designed, built, and flew early dirigibles

Count Zeppelin, who built the first airship with a rigid frame

The third American-built dirigible, and the last, was a sister ship of the *Akron* named the *Macon,* put into service in the summer of 1933 shortly after the *Akron* crashed. Her luck was no better. In fact, the similarities of their destruction were striking. The *Macon* had been in operation about a year and a half when, in February, 1935, she took part in Navy maneuvers off the California coast. Struck by a sudden squall, the *Macon* was thrown out of control when the wind tore off her upper fin. She lurched violently and her tail dropped perilously, tossing crew members in all directions.

"Stand by to abandon ship!" Captain Herbert Wiley ordered.

When the dirigible hit the ocean, some crewmen jumped free through the windows and the rips in her outer surface. Others clung to ropes and broken pieces of framework until rescue ships came. All but two of the eighty-three crewmen escaped, but the *Macon* was only a heap of floating debris. For Captain Wiley, fortune was kind. He was one of the three survivors of the *Akron*; now he got out alive from the *Macon.*

The United States Navy was not destined to fly dirigibles successfully, it seemed.

The Germans in the 1920's were forbidden by the peace terms from building military dirigibles, so they constructed them for commercial use and put them into cross-ocean passenger service. The *Graf Zeppelin* carried passengers and freight on a regular schedule from 1928 until 1937, most of the time between Germany and South America.

The greatest of the dirigibles was the *Hindenburg.* Truly a ship of the sky, this German craft was 804 feet long, high as a fourteen-story building, and carried sixteen gas bags within her body. During 1936, her first year of service, she made ten round trips between Europe and the United States on a fixed schedule. The long-held dream of regular transatlantic aerial passenger service had become a reality, at last. At seventy-five miles an hour, the airship crossed the Atlantic approximately three times as rapidly as the ocean liners did, and without seasickness for the passengers.

Travel on the *Hindenburg* was luxurious. Inside her hull were

The inside of a dirigible. This view shows the aluminum skeleton frame of Count Zeppelin's airship. The photograph was taken in the boathouse, when the airship was only half constructed. It was 420 feet long, in comparison to the Hindenburg's *804-foot length.*

staterooms for seventy passengers on two decks. Outside their cabin doors were lounge areas with big slanting windows looking down on the ocean. These windows, usually kept open, were partially protected by the massive silvery bulk above. A dining room whose tables were set with linen, silver, and fine china occupied one side of the cabin area. Even shower baths, whose water came out in rather thin trickles, were among the conveniences. The smoking room and bar were popular gathering places. Life in flight aboard the *Hindenburg* was much like being on an ocean liner—spacious and congenial, except that the flight was usually calm, quiet, indeed almost serene.

Despite its size and comforts, potential disaster lurked around

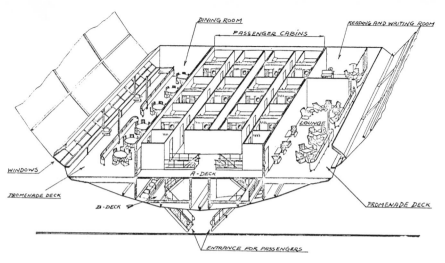

The Hindenburg's *passenger quarters*

the *Hindenburg* every minute she was in the air. Passengers and crew either forgot or ignored the peril.

The danger lay in the hydrogen gas, seven million cubic feet of it, that filled the airship's inflatable cells. While very light, hydrogen is explosive. A spark will make it burst into flame with a terrifying roar. American dirigibles were filled with helium, a gas that will not explode. Since the Germans were unable to obtain helium, they had to use hydrogen. They took every precaution possible to prevent exposure to a spark or flame. When passengers came aboard, for example, they had to turn in their matches and cigarette lighters. The smoking areas of the airship had electric lighters which gave off no flame.

In the first days of May, 1937, the *Hindenburg* flew west across the Atlantic on the first of her eighteen crossings scheduled that summer, her destination as usual the mooring mast at the Lakehurst, New Jersey, Naval Air Station. She carried thirty-six passengers, and a crew of sixty-one which had been enlarged for training purposes.

After gliding past New York City, in late afternoon the *Hindenburg*'s silvery hulk appeared over Lakehurst at an altitude of a few hundred feet. Instead of landing immediately, the airship moved slowly past to the south to avoid gusty rain squalls over the landing site. The wind, always the enemy of dirigibles, would have made the ground crew's job of capturing her ropes and lashing her to the mooring mast most difficult. Several thousand spectators waited at the hangar.

The squall blew itself out, and shortly after 7:00 P.M. the *Hindenburg* nosed down toward the mooring mast, alternately dropping water ballast and letting off hydrogen as her officers "trimmed" the airship. At two hundred feet altitude, her nose was close to the mast. Crewmen tossed coils of landing ropes out the forward hatches. Catching them, the ground crewmen guided the giant toward the mast. All was normal, an impressive spectacle of aerial might under tight control.

Then, suddenly, without warning, fire!

Those on the ground saw flames leap from the top of the dirigible, just in front of the upper fin. Instantly, the back quarter of the *Hindenburg* was a ball of fire. The airship sank toward the ground; the weight of the fall broke its back, and the front end nosed skyward. Within seconds, the front too was swept by

Travelers wait to board the Graf Zeppelin *in the hangar at Lakehurst, New Jersey. It was at Lakehurst that the* Hindenburg *crashed.*

fire and explosions as the gas cells ignited like tremendous fire-crackers. A pillar of orange flame and black smoke rose in the sky.

The ground crew ran for cover, to avoid being crushed. As the blazing broken hull struck the ground, passengers and crew members left from windows and through gashes in the cover. Many had no chance to escape from the pyre.

In less than a minute the *Hindenburg* had been turned from the proudest dirigible of all into a red-hot pile of debris. Thirty-six persons perished, including one member of the ground crew. Amazingly, sixty-two of those aboard survived the holocaust. Among the luckiest was a fourteen-year-old cabin boy, Werner Franz. He jumped to the ground from a hatch in the bottom of the airship, only to find himself being choked by the flames. At that moment, a ballast tank above him burst, drenching him with water and reviving him. He walked through a gap in the framework to safety.

More than the *Hindenburg* and its victims died that night. So did the entire dirigible dream.

Nobody is certain what caused the fatal explosion. Many airship experts suggested possible accidental causes, while a few suggested sabotage. Adolf Hitler and the Nazi Party which controlled Germany were hated by millions of persons for their ruthless seizure of territory from other countries and their persecution of Jews. It is possible, but never proven, that in retaliation someone might have sabotaged the *Hindenburg*, one of Hitler's prides, by firing a bullet into a gas bag.

The *Graf Zeppelin*, also filled with hydrogen, was withdrawn from service immediately. No more dirigibles were ever built.

Smaller, non-rigid blimps have served well in military observation work, and airship enthusiasts talk at times about building airships for freight hauling because they do not need much fuel to operate. But the giants of them all, the passenger-carrying dirigibles, are gone forever. Like the dinosaurs that once roamed the earth, they were impressive but their bulk and slowness made them defenseless against the forces of nature. The skies belonged to the airplane.

— 7 —

Next Stop: Paris

As airplanes became bigger and their engines more reliable in the mid-1920's, audacious aviators began thinking about long-distance flights across the oceans. Those would be the ultimate test of a man's bravery. The result of such a flight would be fame or death. A pilot who lost control or had his engine fail while far out over the ocean almost certainly was doomed.

Most alluring of the long-distance ocean flights pilots dreamed about making was the one between New York and Paris, across the North Atlantic. The distance was great, about 3,600 miles, but so was the reward awaiting the first aviator to fly it nonstop. A prize of $25,000 had been posted by Raymond Orteig, a French hotel operator living in New York, for the one who achieved the goal. Orteig made his offer in 1919, and by mid-1926 no flyer had attempted to win it. During those seven years, even the most daring pilots had considered the risks too great in the planes then available.

During 1926, men on both sides of the Atlantic believed that with a proper new plane and good luck, someone might be able to make the flight. Newspapers argued about the possibility. Soon several flyers announced, "I am going to do it." Their decisions led to an heroic, sometimes tragic, and occasionally laughable competition for glory that became known as "The Great 1927 New York-to-Paris Air Derby."

Paris was a faraway, romantic place to most Americans then.

Roosevelt Field, Long Island, about 1926. New York-to-Paris flight activity centered here.

They had read about the Arc de Triomphe and the Eiffel Tower, the sidewalk cafés and the Place de l'Opera, the cathedral of Notre Dame and the Montmarte section where the artists lived in attics. They had heard tales of Gay Paree from American soldiers in World War I. Not many Americans had visited the French capital, however. Only a relatively few peacetime travelers made the crossing of the Atlantic by ship; that voyage was widely regarded as something of an adventure in itself, to be afforded by those with abundant money and time. The idea of an aviator flying in a single hop between the two great metropolises fascinated everyone.

Those who have sailed on the North Atlantic know that it is an angry ocean. Its gray-green waters are constantly a-churn. Storms stir up long rollers, and towering waves break with a line of foam across their tops, then tumble down into valleys, causing ships to roll and toss. Thick clouds and drizzly belts of fog obscure the sky above the water, often for days. For the airplanes of the time, usually flown at altitudes of only a few thousand feet, the Atlantic was an ominous threat.

Actually, the Atlantic had been flown previously, although almost everyone forgot about this fact during the frantic daily buildup in the newspapers about the possibilities of a New York-to-Paris flight. Within two months during the late spring and early summer of 1919, three flights had been made across the ocean. None of them approached in nonstop duration the distance involved in the New York-to-Paris route.

The very first airplane to cross from North America to Europe under its own power was the United States Navy flying boat NC-4. This was a cumbersome biplane with four motors, three in front pulling and the fourth behind, pushing, of a type intended to be an anti-submarine bomber in World War I but not completed in time. Even with four engines, it could fly only eighty miles an hour. The Navy sent three of these planes on this attempt to span the ocean, believing that both the possibility of success and safety were greater if they flew in formation. A full nonstop crossing of the Atlantic by the lumbering "Nannies," a name the Navy disliked, was impossible. So the plan was to fly from Newfoundland to the Azores, rest there, then fly from those Portuguese islands in the Atlantic to Portugal at the southwestern tip of Europe.

The NC-1, NC-3, and NC-4 took off from the bay at Trepassey, Newfoundland, on May 8, 1919. Each plane had a six-man crew. Soon trouble developed, as it was to do during so many Atlantic flights to follow. The NC-1 was forced down at sea. Her crew was rescued by a ship, but an American destroyer had

The NC-3 was one of the planes the Navy sent to fly across the Atlantic. It was originally intended as an antisubmarine bomber in WWI.

to sink the flying boat so it would not become a hazard to shipping. The NC-4 flew safely to the Azores.

But what had happened to the NC-3? That flying boat didn't reach the Azores, and no word was heard from it by radio. Destroyers searched the stormy sea in vain. A day passed, and another, with no report. The NC-3 was given up for lost.

Then, to the amazement of observers along the breakwater at Porta Delgada, the Azores, the long-overdue flying boat came drifting into harbor, backward. She was barely afloat, her engines dead, with a man standing on each wing strapped to struts for safety in order to hold the leaky flying boat on an even keel.

"It's a miracle!" the nearby United States destroyer *Harding* signaled in Morse code with its flashing lamp. Indeed it was.

The story the NC-3's crew told when they finally reached shore was one of rugged endurance and bravery. The flying boat had been forced down far at sea in a gale, wallowing in waves thirty feet high. Although her hull leaked, she remained afloat. Her radio transmitter was ruined. Helplessly, her crew could hear the signals between searching destroyers but could not respond, "Here we are!"

The only encouraging fact was that navigational readings showed the flying boat drifting on a current eastward toward Porta Delgada.

The NC-3 drifts backward into harbor, Porta Delgada, the Azores.

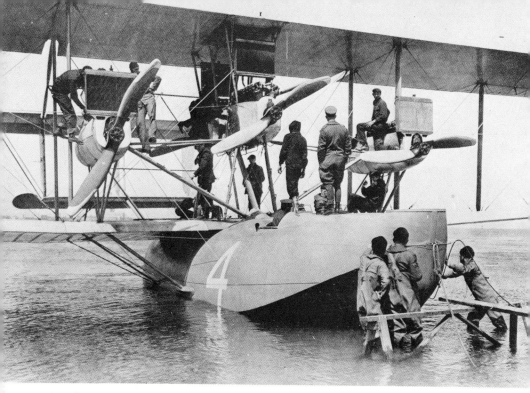

Mechanics work on the NC-4, first airplane to fly across the Atlantic Ocean, the only one of three Navy flying boats to complete the trip.

The six men had little food and were forced to drink rusty water from the radiators. Parts of the plane were battered off by the seas. It became necessary to cut a hole in the sagging wing fabric so accumulated water wouldn't force it under the ocean surface. For sixty hours the helpless flying boat had drifted, until one of the men shouted, "Land—dead astern!" After floating more than two hundred miles, the NC-3 drifted into safe harbor almost foundering but with her American flag waving proudly. She never flew again.

The NC-4, last survivor of the threesome, later flew safely from the Azores to Lisbon, Portugal, and a boisterous European welcome.

Barely two weeks later, two British veterans of World War I, John Alcock and Arthur Whitten Brown, flew the 1,890-mile ocean gap from Newfoundland to Ireland in a two-engined British Vickers Vimy land plane, originally intended as a World War I

Captain René Fonck, France's World War I flying ace, with friends at Roosevelt Field, Long Island, in 1926

bomber. They, too, had a perilous trip through nasty Atlantic weather. Sleet battered their faces when they looked out of the cockpit, and ice formed on the wings. In mid-Atlantic, Brown climbed out onto the lower wing to chip away the ice before the weight of it dragged the plane into the sea. Alcock and Brown landed in an Irish peat bog, nose down, with the plane's tail high in the air, but both escaped safely. Their flight was a truly remarkable achievement. On the heels of their trip, the British dirigible R-34 flew west to New York in early July, completing the trio of crossings.

After that, strangely, the Atlantic remained unchallenged from the air for years. The difference between 1,800 miles from Newfoundland to Ireland and the 3,600-mile flight needed to collect Orteig's New York-to-Paris prize appeared insurmountable.

When the dashing Captain René Fonck announced in Paris in 1926 that he would be the first to try for the Orteig prize, the excitement began. Fonck was France's most honored wartime flying hero, having shot down an amazing total of 125 German planes in combat. How appropriate it was, the French said, that their own legendary hero would be the first to fly between Paris and New York! French honor and pride were aglow.

Fonck was practical, too. He chose to attempt the flight across the Atlantic from west to east, New York to Paris, rather than the other way around, to take advantage of the prevailing eastbound winds. He came to New York by ship and arranged to pilot a Sikorsky S-35 with three engines, built especially for the flight. After months of preparation, he announced that the silver-colored plane, very large for its day, would take off from Roosevelt Field, outside New York City on Long Island, at dawn on September 21. The date was picked so the four-man crew would have the light of the full moon at night over the Atlantic, if the weather happened to be clear.

A runway one mile long and 150 feet wide was cut in the grass of Roosevelt Field for the takeoff. Difficult as it is for us to believe today, accustomed as we are to broad concrete runways and tight airport security, three dirt roads crossed the runway. Spectators were allowed to race their cars along the narrow takeoff path, or to park them close to it. The crossroads provided three bumpy barriers the plane had to bounce over as it made its takeoff run.

Shortly before dawn on that Tuesday morning, Fonck and his three companions arrived at the plane by automobile as the last of 2,500 gallons of gasoline were poured into the tanks. Fonck looked very much the hero in his blue French Army uniform, with ribbons on his chest representing medals he had won in war and shiny brown leather puttees on his legs. Spotlights shone on the under part of the plane, and hundreds of automobile headlights speckled the darkness along the runway.

Charles Clavier, a French member of the crew, gaily said as he climbed aboard, "Dinner in Paris Wednesday night!"

A woman spectator called to Captain Fonck, "*Bon voyage!*" just as at a ship sailing.

"*Merci, madame. Au revoir,*" he replied with a slight bow.

One of the roads that cut through the Roosevelt Field runway in 1926 and jarred loose part of René Fonck's landing gear

At 6:00 A.M. the three engines were started. Fonck revved them up and sent the fourteen-ton plane down the runway, slowly gathering speed. Some motorists drove their cars alongside, hoping for a closeup view of the S-35 leaving the ground.

Halfway down the runway, an ominous sign appeared. The plane was leaving a warning trail of dust. Part of the landing gear had jarred loose when the wheels bumped over one of the crossroads. Fonck needed a speed of eighty miles an hour to get the overloaded plane off the ground. With the broken part dragging, he couldn't get more than sixty-five.

The Frenchman faced a critical decision. The plane had no brakes; no planes did then. If he turned off the runway, he would roll into the sideline crowds. If he cut the engines, he might lose control completely and nose over. So he plunged ahead with throttle wide open. He gambled on gaining air speed in the final few hundred feet of runway—and lost.

At the end of the runway, the plane rolled forward into a twenty-foot gully and vanished from sight. Moments of awful silence followed. Then, a roar as the 2,500 gallons of gasoline exploded in a pillar of flame fifty feet high. While the crowd stood, shocked almost into inaction, Fonck staggered up from the gully, dazed and bedraggled but unhurt. So did Lieutenant Lawrence W. Curtin, the American navigator. Clavier and the fourth crew member, Jacob Islamoff, perished in the flames.

Instead of a triumph, the first attempt to win New York-to-Paris glory ended in disaster. The news dampened the enthusiasm of some for the contest. Yet it only hardened the determination of other aspirants, who said to themselves, "Fonck couldn't do it, but I can!"

During the winter of 1926-27, announcements were made in the United States and France about transatlantic flight projects planned when the "flying season" began the following spring. As the last snow disappeared from Roosevelt Field, five serious contenders emerged.

One was another pair of French war heroes, Captain Charles Nungasser, pilot, and Captain Francis Coli, navigator, who had lost his right eye in the war and wore a black eye patch. These

Richard E. Byrd

two planned to fly west, Paris to New York. Two United States Navy officers, Lieutenant Commander Noel Davis and Lieutenant Stanton H. Wooster, announced a west-to-east attempt. Charles A. Levine, president of the Columbia Aircraft Corporation, said he would enter a monoplane designed by Giuseppe Bellanca. Levine had become wealthy selling surplus military scrap material after World War I and was hungry for publicity. The biggest project of all was headed by an authentic American hero, Lieutenant Commander Richard E. Byrd, who had led history's first flight over the North Pole a year earlier. Byrd had a trimotored Fokker plane; he said he would attempt the New

133

York-to-Paris flight not for the prize money, since he had ample financial backing, but for scientific research. Finally, an application to compete for Orteig's $25,000 arrived signed C.A. Lindbergh.

"Who is he?" the others asked.

"His application says he is an airmail pilot out in Illinois," they were told. That was all anybody knew about him.

As March turned into April, front pages of American newspapers were full of stories about the rival flyers' preparations. The question most frequently asked was, which one of them will take off across the ocean first?

For awhile, Levine's single-engined *Columbia* seemed likely to be the one. He grabbed all the headlines he could by announcing that he had chosen the navigator for the flight, Lloyd Bertaud, but couldn't decide on the pilot between Clarence Chamberlin, an experienced but not very glamorous-looking flyer, and Bert Acosta, who was somewhat better known. Levine told Chamberlin that he didn't doubt his flying ability but was afraid he wouldn't photograph well in the motion pictures the crew would be invited to make after its triumphant landing in Paris!

Amazingly, Levine announced that the choice of pilot would not be made until the last minute before takeoff. "It will then be determined by lot. Both pilots will appear upon the field in flying togs. Their names will be written separately on slips of paper. One slip will be drawn. The name on it will decide the flyer."

What a way to make such a life-and-death decision! As the world was finding out, Levine was full of weird ideas.

The *Columbia* was subject to more unpredictability than Levine had in mind, as it turned out. After a ceremony in which the plane was christened with a bottle of ginger ale, Chamberlin was asked by a guest at the ceremony to take two girls, nine and fifteen years old, for a short flight. During the takeoff, one wheel fell off the plane. Being a skillful pilot, Chamberlin landed the plane on the other wheel, safely, but scraped one wing along the ground. That was on April 24. Weeks of repair work were required.

The America *being prepared outside its hangar on Long Island for its attempted flight from New York to France*

Earlier, Byrd's big Fokker had suffered damage that knocked it out of contention temporarily. On a test flight in New Jersey, the plane proved to be nose-heavy and tipped over while landing. Byrd broke an arm in the crash.

Luck was running poorly for the various entrants. A few days after Levine's plane lost its wheel, tragedy struck. Having named their plane *American Legion* in honor of the veterans organization, Davis and Wooster took it up for a test flight over Virginia on April 26. Fully loaded, the plane rose off the ground a few feet, stalled, and crashed into a swamp. Both men were killed.

Nothing had been heard from that midwestern airmail pilot since he filed his entry form.

All these accidents left the field to the French pair, Nungesser and Coli, for the moment. Their plane was an all-white biplane of French design, a Lavasseur, with a single 450-horsepower engine. They named it the *White Bird*. During late April and the first days of May, French and American newspapers published increasingly excited stories about the imminent takeoff from Le Bourget Field in Paris for the westward crossing. After the sorrow of the Fonck plane's crash the previous fall, French newspapers were especially anxious for Nungesser and Coli to win the glory of being first. Nungesser announced, "I am attempting the flight to bring honor to French aviation"—just the kind of talk the French press loved.

The *White Bird* had one odd feature. Its fuselage was shaped somewhat like a flying boat, sloping up at the front like the prow of a vessel. After it took off from Paris, the crew would release the landing gear to lighten the weight. When they reached New York, their plan was to land the *White Bird* in the water of the harbor, like a great white seagull settling down from a long overwater journey.

Takeoff from Le Bourget was to be at dawn Sunday, May 8. A throng of Parisians including renowned nightclub entertainers gathered after midnight to cheer the departure. As the two airmen walked from an open automobile to the plane, a woman tossed Nungesser a single rose. He caught it and blew her a kiss of gratitude. The *White Bird* used almost the entire runway before it rose reluctantly and headed for the coast, with the first rays of the morning sun reflecting off its wings. A formation of French military planes escorted it for several miles.

Dropping its landing gear as planned, the *White Bird* flew west over southern England, was sighted over Ireland as it headed out over the Atlantic—and was never seen or heard from again. It simply vanished, forever.

Watchers were so eager for Nungesser and Coli to succeed that unfortunately some imagined they had sighted the plane over North America and wrongly sent out the happy word. This resulted in an extremely painful blunder. In Paris, *La Presse* published a special edition on Monday evening with headlines announcing the safe arrival of the *White Bird* in New York Harbor. An imaginative writer had dressed up the false arrival bulletin with graphic details about ships flying welcome flags and escort planes circling as the *White Bird* landed at the foot of the Statue of Liberty—every word false. Parisians were jubilant until a denial had to be issued.

The United States Navy made the situation worse by issuing a bulletin in midafternoon Monday that Nungesser and Coli had been sighted over Portland, Maine. This led some American newspapers to print headlines, FRENCH FLYERS REACH NORTH AMERICA.

By Tuesday, the grim truth had emerged. Nobody had seen the plane. Its gasoline had been exhausted. Frustrated and distressed, Paris newspapers printed a story that Nungesser and Coli had failed because the Americans had withheld vital weather information and permitted them to fly into a heavy storm. This,

Clarence Chamberlin

too, was false. The two Frenchmen had not asked for special
American weather guidance, using the normal weather reports
put out by the United States Navy. Heavy static had prevented
the radio receivers in Paris from hearing the forecast.

Such an anti-American mood developed in the streets and
cafés of Paris that the American ambassador cabled word home
it would be unwise for any American entry in the New York-to-
Paris contest to arrive in the French capital for awhile, for fear
of unfriendly demonstrations.

That didn't halt Charles Levine from announcing that his *Columbia*, now repaired, would take off from New York the end of that week, on Saturday, May 14, with Chamberlin as pilot. Levine's eagerness involved more than his willingness to defy French feelings. Byrd's plane had appeared, almost ready to go. News dispatches from St. Louis reported the imminent arrival in New York of the forgotten man in the competition, Charles A. Lindbergh. The lanky blond pilot about whom so little was known had flown his new Ryan monoplane nonstop from San Diego, California, to St. Louis and was due to arrive at Curtiss Field on Long Island the evening of May 12. Levine wasn't about to let such an unknown longshot start across the Atlantic before his *Columbia*, especially when word came out that Lindbergh intended to fly to Paris alone.

8

The Lone Eagle Triumphs

Excitement became intense around New York after "Slim" Lindbergh's sudden arrival on the scene. Newspapers published daily front page stories about the three rivals poised to attempt the perilous 3,600-mile flight to Paris. On the Sunday after Lindbergh's arrival at Curtiss Field from California, thirty thousand visitors flocked to that airfield and to nearby Roosevelt Field to see the planes and seek glimpses of the men who were about to risk their lives flying them.

In speculation about the competitors' chances, Lindbergh was the last choice. Little was known about him or the Ryan monoplane he was flying, named the *Spirit of St. Louis*.

Byrd was famous for his flight across the North Pole; his tri-motored Fokker plane was the heaviest and largest of the three remaining entrants. Levine's *Columbia* also was widely publicized. Clarence Chamberlin and Bert Acosta had set a world endurance flight record of fifty-one hours, eleven minutes in it a short time earlier, proving that it could fly a long distance. Byrd planned a crew of four on his flight. The *Columbia* would have two men who could relieve each other at the controls.

Lindbergh was alone. No one else would be aboard for companionship and relief at the controls.

"He's crazy," men around the airfield hangars said. "He'll never be able to stay awake that long. Even if his engine doesn't

A replica of Charles A. Lindbergh's Spirit of St. Louis *was built to commemorate the fiftieth anniversary of his flight. Pilot Verne Jobst stands beside it at a stop on its national tour.*

fail, he will doze off and either fall into the sea or get lost and run out of fuel."

They didn't know their man. Going back to those nights on the Chicago–St. Louis airmail run when he conceived the idea of flying the ocean, Lindbergh had calculated every possibility with cool scientific logic. He knew the odds he faced. Everything depended upon him alone; that was the way he wanted it. He believed in himself and his plane and was ready to gamble his life. If his plane had enough powers of endurance, so did he.

The fact that he was at the airfield, ready to take off the moment the weather improved sufficiently, was a result of perseverance and good luck. Six months earlier he had neither an airplane for a long flight nor the money to buy one. When Fonck had crashed on the first New York-to-Paris flight attempt, Lindbergh was unknown beyond his circle of friends along the midwestern airmail route. Now, suddenly, he was the center of so much publicity that it almost overwhelmed him. Reporters clamored to find out about him for their stories. This modest, shy Midwesterner didn't talk about himself readily, nor was he surrounded by friends and helpers. Someone called him the "Lone Eagle," and the name stuck.

The previous winter, he had estimated that he would need $10,000 for a suitable plane. His own savings amounted to $2,000. The rest he hoped to obtain from St. Louis businessmen by convincing them that his flight would publicize their city. He did raise the $10,000; his next task was to find an airplane.

Most of the other transatlantic aspirants either had or were obtaining planes with multiple engines, mostly trimotors, because they considered them safer in case of engine failure. Lindbergh disagreed. One good engine, he reasoned, required only a third as much gasoline and should reduce the peril of a takeoff crash caused by an overload. Also, a multiple-engined plane needed three or more men in its crew, reducing the amount of fuel it could carry.

Finding a plane that met Lindbergh's standards and the size of his bankroll proved difficult. At last he negotiated an arrangement with the little Ryan Airlines, Inc., of San Diego, California, to build a plane for him, made to order for the Atlantic flight. The corporation promised to do the job for $10,000 and to deliver the plane two months from the day the order was signed.

The signing was the end of February. This meant that Lindbergh would have a plane by late April. If any rival got into the air across the Atlantic before then, he could do nothing about it.

The Ryan plant was a ramshackle former fish cannery, near the San Diego waterfront, in which the struggling company built a few planes as orders could be obtained. During those two months, Lindbergh practically lived in the building, working day and night with the designer. As drawings for portions of the plane were finished in the loft workroom, they were handed to

The engine of the Spirit of St. Louis *is started for the first time at the Ryan factory in San Diego. Charles A. Lindbergh stands beside the cockpit window, watching anxiously.*

workmen waiting for them. On one work table Donald Hall, the design engineer, made his drawings. At an adjoining table in the bare room under a single light bulb, Lindbergh plotted his route from New York to Paris. He marked it on an ocean chart he found in a ship supply store.

The two men knew that success lay in having enough fuel aboard to carry the plane over the 3,600-mile route, plus a reserve of four hundred miles, and still building a plane light enough to get off the ground. They worked out a chart showing how many feet of runway the plane would need to become airborne with various loads, including the maximum. It would be close. Equipment that most pilots would regard as important was left off. Every pound counted.

Night-flying equipment was eliminated. So were gasoline

gauges. "I'll measure fuel consumption with my watch," Lindbergh explained. Nor did he carry a parachute, because that would add twenty pounds; he did, however, include an inflatable rubber raft he had seen in a store window. The flight was to be made without a radio or navigating instruments because the pilot considered a few more gallons of gasoline more important.

Thus the *Spirit of St. Louis* emerged from the Ryan plant in late April as a spartan, lovingly built airplane of precision craftsmanship that embodied Lindbergh's flying theories and his belief in simplicity. He talked about the plane almost as though it were a person, referring to "We."

The plane's nose was sheathed with aluminum, but the fuselage was covered by fabric drawn tight. Like other planes of the period, it had fixed landing wheels, which were a drag on its speed. Nor was there an automatic pilot; Lindbergh had to have one hand on the control stick every moment or the plane drifted off course.

Most inconvenient of all was the pilot's inability to see straight ahead while seated in his cockpit wicker chair. Space had to be made in front of the pilot for an extra gasoline tank. This gave the plane the necessary balance but blocked the pilot's view. Either he had to look out the side windows or through a homemade periscope consisting of a tube and two mirrors that could be extended through the left side of the fuselage. By peering through this contraption, Lindbergh could see what lay immediately ahead.

His cockpit was so cramped that he could touch the fuselage wall on either side by extending his elbows. When a liquid compass was installed in New York, it had to be placed on the ceiling of the cockpit, where Lindbergh had to read it backward. He solved this when a young woman at the airfield gave him the small mirror from her compact. He stuck the mirror onto the instrument panel with chewing gum, and through the mirror he could read the compass course.

As his own plane took shape, Lindbergh read uneasily about the progress of his rivals, all of whom had their planes near the starting points on the East Coast or in Paris, while he was far away and unnoticed in Southern California. They seemed so close to taking off that sometimes he almost despaired. As he waited in San Diego for good weather so he could fly his plane to New York, he read about Nungesser and Coli's departure from Paris, and then their disappearance. While sorrowing at their tragedy, he knew that he still had a chance.

The *Spirit of St. Louis* first took to the air at San Diego on April 18, and Lindbergh was pleased with its performance. More days passed while final adjustments were made. The first moment he could, Lindbergh took off from San Diego almost unnoticed. Only after he arrived in St. Louis after the longest nonstop solo flight ever made, paused briefly, and sped on to New York did his name make headlines. His days of being unknown were finished for the rest of his life.

The period that followed Lindbergh's arrival at Curtiss Field on the evening of May 12 was hectic. The arrival of this handsome 25-year-old bachelor pilot fascinated the crowds and the newspapers. He seemed so boyish and bashful. A reporter for the New York *Times* wrote, "No one ever more perfectly personified youthful adventure than this young knight of the air." Describing the scene outside the hangar in which the *Spirit of St. Louis* was being serviced, he added, "There were many girls in the crowd who watched the good-looking pilot with undisguised admiration. Lindbergh seems to be girl-shy, but they 'simply adore' him." Some girls sent messages to him, asking that he take them along to Paris.

While the *Columbia* crew, Byrd's *America* men, and Lindbergh were gracious to each other, they were wary. Rumors circulated about their plans, often suggesting that once the bad weather broke over the Atlantic, two or even all three might take off simultaneously and race across. A week passed. Everyone was on edge but discouraged by seemingly endless reports of storms and fog over the ocean.

On Thursday evening, May 19, after a long day around the airfield, Lindbergh agreed to drive with friends from Long

144

Island into Manhattan for relaxation, to see the Broadway musical *Rio Rita*. They stopped at the Weather Bureau for the latest report and to their surprise found that conditions over the Atlantic were clearing. A weather front was moving east from Long Island and New England over the ocean, leaving mostly clear skies behind it.

"Let's get back to the airfield. I'm going to take off tomorrow morning," Lindbergh said.

Instead of seeing *Rio Rita* they hurried back to Curtiss Field, arriving there about midnight. After arranging for a final tune-up of the plane's engine, Lindbergh tried to get two and a half hours' sleep in a nearby hotel. Even his usual calm was affected by tension, however, and he tossed restlessly.

Shortly before 3:00 A.M. he arrived at the Curtiss Field hangar. The clouds were low and a light rain fell, hardly the kind of weather that seemed right for takeoff. Lindy looked over to the *Columbia*, expecting to see its crew also making preparations, and was surprised at the lack of activity. Either they hadn't heard the weather report or had difficulty of some kind.

When fully loaded, the *Spirit of St. Louis* was too heavy to take off from Curtiss Field. It had to be moved to the larger Roosevelt Field a short distance away. But how, at this black, predawn hour? Lindbergh's decision to go had been so sudden that no arrangements had been made. Someone offered a truck. About 5:00 A.M. the *Spirit of St. Louis* was pulled out of the hangar and its tail skid lifted into the truck. Five motorcycle policemen escorted the plane as it was towed backward across the bumpy field and along a dirt track to the Roosevelt runway. There Lindbergh saw his other rival, the *America*, parked. Some of its crew were gathered, but they were merely planning another short test flight. Byrd had decided against risking a takeoff that morning.

So it was to be Lindbergh only. Ground crewmen poured 451 gallons of gasoline into the plane's tanks, five gallons at a time from cans. He placed five sandwiches, two canteens of water, and a vacuum jar of coffee in the cockpit—not much food for a thirty-

Pilot about to gas up his early airplane. Note home-made strainer for impurities. Ground crewmen poured 451 gallons of gasoline into Lindy's plane from five gallon cans, one can at a time.

five hour span aloft, but all he wanted.

As the moist dawn came, men in raincoats huddled around the plane, sidestepping puddles. Two of them helped Lindbergh put on his heavy flying suit. At the other end of the mile-long strip of damp, sandy clay, telephone wires stretched across the field's border. To offset the drag caused by the sticky runway surface and the weight of two and a half tons, Lindbergh rubbed the tires with grease. Even such a small detail could mean the difference between a safe takeoff and a fatal crash at the end of the runway. René Fonck's plane had smashed up on this same runway a few months earlier.

A slight tail wind ruffled the sullen atmosphere. Lindbergh's crucial moment had come.

146

Once he started down the runway, his life would hang on his ability to coax the reluctant, overloaded plane into the air before it ran out of ground space. He thought about the charts he and Donald Hall had made back in San Diego, showing how many feet of runway the *Spirit of St. Louis* should need to become airborne when fully loaded. They hadn't calculated on a muddy runway.

A crowd of hundreds had gathered, among them Byrd and Chamberlin, who shook Lindbergh's hand and wished him good luck.

Settling into the cockpit, Lindy raced the motor until the frame of the plane shook. He called out the window to a mechanic, "How is it?"

"Sounds good to me."

Charles A. Lindbergh and the Spirit of St. Louis

"Well, then, I might as well go." Casually he waved, "So long."

A mechanic pulled out the wooden chocks that held the wheels in place, men pushed on the plane's struts to get it rolling, and the *Spirit of St. Louis* lumbered down the runway.

To Lindbergh, and to those watching, it seemed as though the plane never would gain sufficient speed to become airborne. As he passed the safety point, the last chance to turn back, it still showed no signs of pulling free from the earth. The seconds passed, and more runway disappeared behind its wheels. Then a bump in the runway, and the plane lifted a few feet above the earth, only to touch down again almost immediately. Once more it rose and settled to earth. At what seemed like almost the last possible second, the wheels left the ground for the third time—and stayed aloft!

It was almost as though Lindbergh in his grim determination had actually pulled the plane aloft by will power. By a margin of only ten feet, its wheels cleared a tractor at the end of the runway, then skimmed above the telephone wires by twenty feet.

The time was 7:52 A.M. Lindbergh was on his way.

Foot by foot, yard by yard, the *Spirit of St. Louis* gained altitude until it was a hundred feet in the air, high enough to pass above the trees on the golf course that lay ahead, and over the tops of houses beyond.

Once aloft, Lindbergh settled down to his lonely routine. He had chosen to fly the great circle route, rather than head directly across the Atlantic toward Paris. Because of the curvature of the earth, it is shorter to fly northeastward to Boston, Nova Scotia, and Newfoundland before moving out over the open ocean, then curve southeastward approaching Europe.

He was flying by dead reckoning. That is, instead of taking instrument soundings to determine his location en route, he had marked the route he was to fly on the map he held in his lap, in hundred-mile segments. The necessary changes of course were indicated at these points. As he passed over Boston, Nova Scotia, and Newfoundland, he checked his locations by landmarks and

USA·13c

50th Anniversary Solo Transatlantic Flight

U.S. Postal Service stamp commemorating the fiftieth anniversary of Lindbergh's New York-to-Paris flight was issued in May, 1977.

found himself almost precisely on course. His navigation was as precise as his piloting.

Sometimes Lindbergh flew barely ten feet above the water, just high enough that the wheels didn't touch the wave tops. This was to make use of the cushion of smooth air that is found near the water, and thus save fuel. When storm clouds piled up ahead, he piloted the *Spirit of St. Louis* to a 10,000-feet altitude and even higher in an effort to rise above the billowing thunderheads. He sought to pick his way around these clouds, not always successfully.

Darkness fell as he flew over St. Johns, Newfoundland, and out to sea. A long night of monotony and peril stretched ahead. The plane was encased in blackness, a tiny island of metal and fabric bearing a single human being suspended above the ocean. No radio, no signals, no night-lights tied it to the rest of the world. Inside, the cockpit was without electric light, and Lindbergh sat in darkness as intense as that surrounding the aircraft. He could barely see the phosphorescent numerals on the instrument panel. To make hourly entries in his log, he flicked on his flashlight and it nearly blinded him. Once, when he needed to study his navigation markings on the chart, he spread it on his knees while holding the stick between his legs and the flashlight with his chin. Cotton placed in his ears to dull the sound of the engine added to his sense of aloneness.

Sleepiness became his worst enemy. Hour after hour, surrounded by fog and mist, he found his senses dulled from staring at the instruments. He found his eyelids drooping, his mind floating into daydreams. Subconsciously he told himself, "I must stay awake. . . . I must stay awake." With a jolt, he would straighten up and find that he had drifted off course.

At ten thousand feet in clammy clouds during the middle of the night, Lindbergh realized instinctively that something wasn't right. Putting a hand out the window, he felt pinpoint stabs of pain. Ice! Icing of the wings, which froze the controls and added dangerous weight to the plane, was a dreaded peril for early-day aviators, especially those who flew at night. Lindbergh's flashlight beam revealed the frozen formation on the wing. As rapidly as possible, he guided the plane down almost to the sea again, where warmer air melted the ice.

Dawn came, at last, and the *Spirit of St. Louis* droned steadily on, its engine never missing a beat. Only gray tossing ocean was visible, and Lindbergh worried that he had drifted off course during the night. The twenty-four hour mark in the flight passed; he had been sitting in the pilot's seat, feet on the rudder, hand on the stick, for an entire day without moving. Slowly the hours dragged by. The fact that they were uneventful was a portent of success, but the monotony left him glassy-eyed with fatigue.

Then, in mid-afternoon of his second day in the air, the glorious sight he had longed for so long: land!

Lindbergh knew that he had reached the European side of the Atlantic. But precisely where was he, and how far off course? His comparison of the chart and the features of the coastline over which he was flying showed a remarkable thing: he was over Dingle Bay, Ireland, less than three miles from the route he had drawn on that map weeks earlier in San Diego!

From then on, the perils of the flight receded. He was wide

The throng gathered around Charles Lindbergh's plane at Croydon Airport, London, indicates the tremendous enthusiasm his transatlantic flight created. He flew to England from France a few days after his historic landing at Paris.

awake, his mind and eyes keen with anticipation. Over Ireland, over the southwestern tip of England, over the English Channel the *Spirit of St. Louis* flew steadily ahead at a hundred miles an hour, like a homing pigeon headed unswervingly for its roost. As darkness fell for the second time during the flight, Lindbergh crossed the coast of France at the mouth of the River Seine and entered the last lap to Paris. To celebrate, he pulled a sandwich from the brown bag and ate it, the first food he had touched in thirty-three hours aloft.

Above brightly lighted Paris, he circled the Eiffel Tower in

Grinning Charles A. Lindbergh displays joking sign hung in front of the Spirit of St. Louis *by the Ryan Aircraft workers who built it.*

a salute to victory, then pointed the plane's nose northeast to where he believed Le Bourget Airfield lay. The flickering movement of hundreds of lights around the edge of the field puzzled him. Was the city having some kind of disturbance?

He touched the wheels to the ground and taxied to the hangar apron. Paris! He had done it, in thirty-three hours, thirty minutes. As he switched off the engine, he was engulfed in a frantic mob of greeters.

"I'm Charles Lindbergh," he told them. As if they didn't know!

In response, they tossed him into the air in triumph. Those lights had been from automobiles whose owners sped to the airfield when word circulated that the Lone Eagle was approaching. In that instant, Lindbergh became a world hero.

Fifty years later in 1977, on the golden anniversary of Lindbergh's flight, his country honored his memory—he had died a short time previously—by issuing a *Spirit of St. Louis* stamp. The plane is on display in the National Air and Space Museum of the Smithsonian Institution in Washington, where visitors marvel that an aircraft so tiny and fragile, when judged by today's standards, could make such an epic flight.

Flying enthusiasts built a replica of the *Spirit of St. Louis* on the fiftieth anniversary and toured the country with it. Those who flew in this reproduction agreed, "I don't see how he did it. The plane is the roughest and hardest to handle of any plane I've flown." That was the way Lindbergh wanted the controls, rough, so the effort of handling them would keep him awake.

Those who wish to visit Roosevelt Field, from which he took off that rainy morning, are disappointed. The airfield is a shopping mall now. The mall has a plaque describing the event, headed, "HISTORY HAPPENED HERE. Let all who read this remember..."

— 9 —

The Flying Junkman

Charles A. Lindbergh's triumphant flight left Commander Byrd's trimotored Fokker, *America*, and the *Columbia*, owned by Charles A. Levine and piloted by Clarence Chamberlin, grounded at the starting line. Byrd said his plane needed more tests. The *Columbia* stayed behind because Levine was quarreling with its crew. He always seemed to be quarreling with someone.

While Lindbergh was the cool, lone hero of the transatlantic competition, Levine was the "character." As brave as he was unpredictable, the millionaire scrap-metal dealer became involved in antics so ridiculous and yet so dangerous that the world was uncertain whether to laugh at him or cheer him on. Newspapers called him the "Flying Junkman." About all he had in common with Lindbergh was his first name and the initials C.A.L.—that and Atlantic fever.

Levine relished the publicity that swirled around his on-again, off-again decisions about what two men would fly the *Columbia* to Europe. He was determined that his plane would go, even after Lindbergh got there first. There was enough glory left. He himself was not a qualified pilot, although he had taken a few lessons. But he soon would demonstrate the truth in the saying that "a little knowledge is a dangerous thing."

Chamberlin on the other hand was a quiet ex-barnstorming pilot with much experience flying the Bellanca-Wright monoplane Levine had bought and named *Columbia*. Levine had to

154

give up his plan to decide by lot at the last moment whether the plane's pilot would be Chamberlin or Bert Acosta, because Acosta didn't like such erratic behavior when his life was at stake. He quit Levine and joined Byrd's crew. That left Chamberlin as pilot and Bertaud as navigator. Apparently Chamberlin had grown better looking in Levine's eyes as the weeks passed. Levine had him and Bertaud sign agreements giving Levine a share of the money they might earn from vaudeville appearances and writing if they crossed the Atlantic successfully.

By May 13, the *Columbia* was ready to go, but superstitious Levine canceled the takeoff because it was Friday the thirteenth. Then he had another quarrel, this time with navigator Bertaud. Bertaud went to court to prevent the *Columbia* from taking off without him. The judge ruled for Levine, who immediately fired Bertaud. It was almost as confusing as the Abbott and Costello comedy routine, "Who's on first?"

By that time, Lindbergh had flown to Paris and renown.

Two more weeks passed, marked by bad weather. Once Chamberlin had his flying suit on, so close was he to takeoff, only to have the flight postponed. Levine told the press that the *Columbia* was about to fly to Europe. Where in Europe? He wouldn't say. Who would fly with Chamberlin as co-pilot and navigator? That was a secret.

"The second man will be disclosed just before the *Columbia* leaves," he said.

Levine's strange behavior turned the crowds at the airfield against him. They accused him of poor sportsmanship and crude conduct, with reason. Finally, the weather cleared and Chamberlin announced that he would take off for somewhere in Europe at dawn the next day. During the night the plane's fuel tanks were filled and it was towed to the Roosevelt Field runway, just as Lindbergh's had been. This time the runway was dry.

When dawn came on June 4, the spectators gathered around the *Columbia* at the head of the runway witnessed a scene that left them astounded.

Dressed in golf knickers, Chamberlin climbed into the pilot's seat, ready to take off. The motor throbbed noisily. The last

155

moment had arrived but the navigator, whoever he might be, had not. His seat in the cockpit was empty. Mrs. Levine stood at the front of the crowd, behind the ropes, but her husband was nowhere in sight.

Chamberlin turned toward the crowd, smiled, and beckoned. From behind a clump of spectators, where he had been hiding, a short, partly bald man in a business suit, clutching charts, emerged, ran to the plane, and climbed aboard. It was Levine!

He sat down in the navigator's seat, staring straight ahead. On the ground below, his wife watched in amazement. The chief of the ground crew ran over and told her, "It's just a test run. They are only going down the runway a few hundred feet."

At that moment, Chamberlin roared the engine and the *Columbia* rolled down the runway. Everyone but Mrs. Levine thought it was taking off. Part way down the runway the plane stopped, turned around and taxied back to the starting point.

What strange behavior, everyone except Mrs. Levine thought. She knew Chamberlin was coming back to let her husband off the plane. At least, she thought she knew.

Back at the head of the runway, Chamberlin turned the *Columbia* downfield again, poured power to the engine, and without a pause rumbled down the path at gathering speed for takeoff.

Realizing that her husband was still aboard, Mrs. Levine screamed, "Oh-h-h! He's not going? He's not going?" As the *Columbia* left the ground smoothly, headed for Europe, she staggered into the arms of a policeman and collapsed.

Levine had planned for a long time to be the second man aboard but didn't dare say so. He was brave enough for the perilous flight but lacked the nerve to face his wife. Once, when she heard him say jokingly that maybe he should go with Chamberlin, she had retorted that she would burn the plane if she thought he was serious about the idea. After he was well on his way, she was handed a letter he had left for her, explaining what he was doing.

Only Chamberlin had known Levine's plan, and he didn't tell.

The Bellanca monoplane Columbia *being tested by Clarence Chamberlin and Bert Acosta at Roosevelt Field in 1927*

The pilot hardly could afford to, because Levine was paying him $25,000 to fly him to Europe.

Since Levine couldn't navigate and knew very little about piloting, he became the first passenger on a transatlantic flight attempt. He did relieve Chamberlin at the controls occasionally, so Chamberlin could take brief naps on top of the large fuel tank behind the *Columbia's* cockpit. This made the flight less of a strain on the pilot than Lindbergh's solo trip.

The *Columbia* flew approximately the same great circle route that Lindbergh used and was blessed with better weather. Although they didn't say so in advance, Chamberlin and Levine had set Berlin as their destination. They would have been satisfied with any landing in Europe beyond Paris, so they could outdo Lindbergh's distance record. But their compass failed, and as they droned across the Atlantic on their second day in the air, they weren't sure where England was.

To their delight, they saw the ocean liner *Mauretania* steaming westward below them. They happened to have a copy of the previous morning's New York *Times* aboard. By checking the shipping table in the newspaper, they found that the *Mauretania* had sailed from Cherbourg, France, yesterday and therefore must be about 350 miles from the French coast. Chamberlin circled the liner so those below could identify the plane. Then he flew a few hundred yards west of the ship, turned the airplane to the east, and went straight along the *Mauretania's* wake. By this off-the-cuff bit of navigation, he knew the *Columbia* was headed directly toward the French coast, from which the ship had come, about three and a half flying hours away.

A few miles farther, the aviators looked down on a westbound United States Navy cruiser, the *Memphis*, which was carrying Lindbergh home.

The luck that had been so kind to Chamberlin and Levine on their takeoff and flight turned sour after they crossed the French coast about twilight. They flew into heavy clouds on their path to Berlin. Trying to get above them, Chamberlin took the plane up to twenty thousand feet, but the foggy overcast persisted. Some of their instruments failed. In truth, they were lost somewhere above Europe. Worried about the mountains he thought must be below, Chamberlin decided to cruise back and forth at high altitude until morning, then seek an opening in the clouds. He was so exhausted that he turned the controls over to Levine with the instruction, "Just hold her steady," and curled up on top of the gas tank.

Suddenly, while he was dozing, the veteran pilot's subconscious instincts told him that something drastic was wrong. He leaped up, frightened. Levine had lost control of the plane, it had stalled, and it was falling toward earth in a spiral. The *Columbia's* controls wobbled wildly. Its frame shook "like a bucking bronco," Chamberlin said later. The altimeter had broken, so they didn't know how high they were. They might crash into the earth at any moment, for all they knew.

Chamberlin applied every ounce of strength and flying skill he had acquired in his long career and finally got the *Columbia* leveled off at four thousand feet altitude. They had fallen three miles!

When daylight came, their third dawn in the air, they dropped below the clouds and found themselves over the German Ruhr. The city below was Dortmund. They circled low over its air-

Clarence Chamberlin, in golf knick-
ers, shakes hands with Charles A.
Levine in front of the plane in
which they made their hectic flight
from New York to Germany.

field, and spectators there collectively pointed their fingers to
the east, toward Berlin. Chamberlin followed those fingers—
another form of navigation that isn't taught in school—and flew
on toward Berlin 350 miles ahead.

With their gasoline almost exhausted, they knew that they
must land soon. When the engine sputtered and coughed, Chamberlin turned it off and glided the *Columbia* into the smoothest-
looking field he could find. This proved to be a wheatfield, whose
owner was torn between feeling honored at having history's longest flight end on his farm and being angry at the damage to his
crop. He spoke no English and they virtually no German. By
sign language, the wandering flyers managed to obtain twenty
gallons of gasoline. Since no funnel was available, the fuel had
to be poured into the tank a quart at a time from a teapot.

After taking off from the wheatfield for the last hundred miles
to Berlin, Chamberlin and Levine somehow managed to miss

the German capital entirely. While crowds waited to greet them, they flew past the city to the south and found themselves headed for Poland. They remembered passing an airfield marked Cottbus, so they turned the *Columbia* around and flew back toward it. Before reaching Cottbus they ran out of gas, again. This time they landed in a muddy pasture and plowed a parallel pair of trenches across it with the plane's wheels. The *Columbia* nosed over in the mud, breaking off the end of a propellor blade. Berlin remained elusive, sixty miles distant.

As if this wasn't indignity enough, the force of the nose-down landing shook loose a box of emergency rations. This broke open, covering Chamberlin with white powdered milk and powdered chocolate. He looked more like a walking malted milk than a hero.

The next day, after a replacement propellor was brought from Berlin, the *Columbia* was towed from the pasture to a nearby football field, and Chamberlin made a risky takeoff to Cottbus. From there, finally, the wandering aviators flew to Tempelhof Airdrome at Berlin and an exuberant welcome. They had, after all, set a new long distance flight record of 3,911 miles in the forty-two hours and forty-five minutes they were airborne from New York to their wheatfield landing.

This isn't the end of the wildly muddled *Columbia* adventures, however. Levine the unpredictable had some weird antics in store.

After an enthusiastically received tour of Central European cities, the two men flew in the *Columbia* to Le Bourget in Paris. Chamberlin had had enough and headed back to the United States by ship. But Levine, having tasted glory in Europe, thought there would be even greater triumphs awaiting him in the United States if the *Columbia* made a return flight across the Atlantic from Europe to New York with him aboard. That would make him the first round-trip Atlantic flyer.

Since he still wasn't a qualified pilot, he engaged a prominent French airman, Maurice Drouhin, to pilot the *Columbia* while he rode along. What did it matter that the two men didn't speak each other's language and had to converse through an interpreter

160

or wiggle their hands at each other in sign language?

Levine's genius for picking arguments soon upset things again. Somehow he got the idea that Drouhin planned to take off without him, so he removed some essential parts from the plane to make that impossible. Drouhin then got a judge to rule that the *Columbia* was forbidden to take off unless he was at the controls.

For days the famous plane sat at Le Bourget under police guard. Nobody knew what would happen next. One day in late August Levine told his wife, who had joined him in Paris, that he was going out to the airfield and check on the *Columbia*. He told the police guard and a mechanic he wanted to taxi the plane around the field, to keep it limbered up. They helped him push it out of the hangar.

Levine taxied the *Columbia* to the far end of Le Bourget, then unexpectedly turned it down the runway, gunned the motor, and took off in a wobbly manner. He had stolen his own plane! Two of Drouhin's friends jumped into another plane and took off in pursuit. When he threatened to ram them in midair, they gave up. Without a map, Levine aimed in the general direction of England.

Word of his approach was cabled across the English Channel. British officials guessed that he was heading for Croydon Aerodrome at London and placed an ambulance and fire engine in readiness at the field. Other planes were ordered to stay clear of the runway, and with cause.

The *Columbia* approached Croydon—Levine somehow had found the field—and came down for a landing. Airport officials blew a siren to warn everyone of his coming. Bringing the plane safely to the ground was more difficult than getting it into the air. Levine couldn't do it. He kept the plane too high and was still five feet above the ground as he neared the far end of the runway. He zoomed back into the air, made a foolhardy climbing turn, barely skimmed over a building, and circled back for another try. Again he went the length of the runway without getting the wheels onto earth. By now the crowd was frantic, even if he wasn't. As he swung around for a third attempt, an English pilot took off in a small plane to guide him. Flying alongside Levine, he beckoned him to follow. The small plane descended with the *Columbia* coming behind. The guide eased his plane to earth, then quickly swung his craft off the runway and behind a hangar as Levine wobbled in behind him. The *Columbia* touched down, bounced thirty feet in the air, bounced again, and finally came to a safe stop.

Reporting the escapade the next morning, the London *Times* commented, "The arrival and subsequent landing by Mr. Levine on Croydon Aerodrome was the most alarming experience which has happened in the memory of the civil aviation traffic officers, regular pilots and aerodrome staff."

Levine didn't seem alarmed. When relieved Englishmen ran up to welcome him, he merely said, "Hello, I think I need a shave. I didn't know I was coming till I almost started."

A British official replied, "You have had a shave—a very close one." Then he led Levine off to an office to tell him how many laws he had broken.

Undaunted, Levine kept talking about the flight he was going to make back to the United States, but he never did it. Eventually he went home by ship, as did the *Columbia*.

That left only Commander Byrd's *America* at Roosevelt Field in New York, waiting to challenge the Atlantic. Of the three planes, it was the largest with three motors and a crew of four. Also, Byrd was the most cautious, preparing for the flight as if for a business operation. He and his backers said their goal was not so much being first as it was exploring the possibility of passenger flights across the Atlantic.

That didn't satisfy some impatient Americans, who wrote to Byrd calling him nasty names and suggesting that he was being cowardly. This was the same man they had welcomed home jubilantly as a hero after his plane had flown over the North Pole.

Finally, on June 29, more than a month after Lindbergh's flight, the *America* took off for Paris. Its crew consisted of Byrd, who commanded the flight but was not a pilot; two pilots, Bernt Balchen and Bert Acosta; and a navigator, George Noville. De-

Bernt Balchen

spite its large crew and good equipment, the *America* lacked an important ingredient for transatlantic flights, good luck. After nearly two days in the air, the trimotored plane finally reached the French coast, 250 miles off course. Its compasses had gone bad, and it ran into fog over France. The crew became lost and wandered above the Continent in an overcast.

As they fumbled along, they saw a revolving light. Byrd assumed that it was Le Bourget and that they had reached Paris. With Balchen at the controls, the *America* came in for a landing, only to have the crew discover that the light they saw wasn't the airport but a lighthouse on the French coast! Their fuel was

163

Richard E. Byrd's America *floats in the Atlantic Ocean off the French coast after a forced landing while attempting a transatlantic flight.*

almost gone. They had to get down to earth quickly. But where could they land their big plane in the darkness? Not blindly in a blackened field, they reasoned, or even on the beach, because of obstacles probably lurking there. They decided to come down in the sea, offshore. Dropping flares, the plane came in low and settled into the water with a thud. All four men were thrown free.

They swam around the plane, calling to each other in the dark, until all four climbed aboard the back of the wing. The front edge was under water. Miraculously, all had survived without serious injury. One of them crawled inside the *America* and pulled out its rubber raft. The men inflated it and paddled the few yards to shore. It wasn't exactly a glorious arrival, but the *America* had flown the Atlantic and landed in France, barely. The men found themselves at the little seaside town of Ver-sur-mer. Later, when the tide was out and the *America* was above the water line, villagers helped the crew pull it ashore.

The great New York-to-Paris Air Derby of 1929 was over. All three planes had flown the Atlantic—Lindbergh triumphantly, Chamberlin and Levine half comically, and Byrd with more than his share of bad luck.

Byrd's talk about seeing transatlantic aerial passenger service established some day came true, of course, but not until twelve years later. More perilous pioneer flights were to be made, such

Passengers on the second transatlantic passenger flight come ashore at Lisbon, Portugal, from the Pan American Dixie Clipper that carried them from New York on June 28, 1939. BELOW: *Pan American Clipper, a Boeing B-314, taking off.*

as Amelia Earhart's trip in 1928 as the first woman to fly the ocean, and more lives of venturesome aviators were to be lost before that day came. At last, in June, 1939, the Pan American Clippers, four-engine flying boats, began regular transatlantic passenger service from New York to Europe. Three months later, World War II broke out.

— 10 —

The Race to Hawaii

As the giant 747 jetliner approached Honolulu in the late 1970's, green Diamond Head glided by on the right, then sunny Waikiki Beach and its line of skyscraper hotels. Passengers stretched their necks to look out at the Hawaiian mountains flecked with clouds, while the plane made a turn and settled its bulk softly on the airport runway.

Barely four hours earlier the jetliner had crossed the California coast of the Pacific Ocean, headed west for open sea. The plane had been cruising at an altitude of more than seven miles, so high that hardly anyone aboard remembered they were flying across 2,400 miles of ocean. That was easy to forget. Stewardesses in long Hawaiian dresses had served dinner. The passengers, more than three hundred of them, listened to stereo music on headsets, watched a movie, and strolled along the two corridors. The cabin was so spacious that they were seated nine abreast.

"I'll tell you about our islands," a cabin attendant said on the public address system. He described the geography, the old Hawaiian kingdom, and the creation of the islands as the fiftieth state.

An old-time Honolulu resident, coming back from the mainland, mumbled to his seatmate, "He should have told about the Dole Derby. That would have made them appreciate this more."

Indeed it would have. The Dole Derby in 1927 from mainland United States to the Hawaiian Islands was the most bizarre

167

Charles A. Lindbergh chats with the famous humorist Will Rogers a few months after his transatlantic flight. Behind them is a trimotored Ford transport plane. Notice the small window.

and tragic race of aviation's Frantic Twenties. To the winner went a prize of $25,000, and to the second place finisher $10,000. Not only was the overwater flight extremely long for the planes of a half century ago, but the flyers' course had to be straight and true so they could hit the small midocean target.

News of Lindbergh's Atlantic flight excited the Hawaiian pineapple king, James D. Dole, who dreamed of the day when airplanes would be flying the Pacific. Four days after Lindbergh landed in Paris, Dole announced that he would sponsor a trans-pacific race to Honolulu and hoped that Lindbergh would enter it. The first plane to reach Honolulu nonstop after August 15, 1927, would collect the $25,000, providing that the feat was accomplished within a year after that starting date.

Lindbergh was too busy touring the United States to enter the Dole contest. Other aviators were ready to take the gamble, however. So many expressed interest that Dole decided upon a mass start. All planes entered were to line up at the Oakland, California, airport on the eastern side of San Francisco Bay and take off one after the other.

Dole announced his offer May 25. This gave the entrants less than three months to prepare.

Twenty-five thousand dollars! That was a very large sum to most of the entrants, who had been earning uncertain incomes as barnstormers and stunt men, or small salaries as junior military officers. They had to obtain suitable planes and backers to pay for them. Naturally, they turned to "booster" businessmen in big cities who were impressed by the publicity St. Louis was receiving because a few men there had helped pay for Lind-bergh's plane. Thus several of the Dole entrants bore such names as *Dallas Spirit, Oklahoma, City of Peoria, Angel of Los Angeles,* and *Aloha* for the plane representing Hawaii.

Fifteen pilots entered the Dole contest—a casual, daredevil lot of men, none of them experienced in long-distance flying. Their planes were as much a mixed bag as the flyers were— mostly monoplanes, a few biplanes, and even one triplane. One hundred miles an hour was a high speed for the planes, which meant that each one completing the flight would be in the air for more than twenty-four hours. Once the planes flew west from the Golden Gate of San Francisco, there was no place for them to land en route except in the ocean.

Looking back, we see how unprepared for the race most of the entrants were. They seemed to assume that bravery was enough,

Poor, pretty Mildred Doran, the only woman in the Dole Derby, who flew in a plane named for her

brushing aside the shortcomings of their planes and the inaccuracy of their instruments. If Lindbergh could do it over the Atlantic, they could do it over the Pacific and become heroes, too.

When it became apparent that Lindbergh wouldn't enter, Dole, who had expected that he would, set the takeoff date from the Oakland airport for August 12. The pilots, having drawn lots for starting positions, were to leave down the unpaved runway a minute or two apart.

Soon the race had a heroine, a pretty one. Her name was Mildred Doran, a 22-year-old schoolteacher from Flint, Michigan. The idea of being the first woman to fly across the Pacific sounded much more exciting than her job of conducting fifth grade in the small nearby town of Caro. She agreed to be the third person, a passenger, in the *Miss Doran*, a plane purchased by a wealthy Flint man and named for her. With one attractive young woman among twenty-five men, much of the publicity naturally focused on her.

As the starting date approached, things began to go wrong. Two of the fifteen entrants withdrew. That left thirteen planes and twenty-six persons. Before the race was over, ten of those twenty-six competitors would be dead. Only four of them would reach the finish line at Wheeler Field, Honolulu. No wonder the race was denounced by many voices as an ill-conceived adventure that should never have been allowed to take place!

Like the ten little Indians, the number of entrants continued to decrease as mishap followed mishap. Two United States Navy officers from San Diego who had entered a plane died when it crashed during a test flight. The pride of Los Angeles, which had two planes entered bearing its name, was humbled when the *Angel of Los Angeles* crashed in a trial, killing the pilot, and the triplane *Pride of Los Angeles* fell into San Francisco Bay five days before the race. Of the original fifteen entrants, three planes had crashed, two had withdrawn, and another never showed up or officially withdrew.

The supervisors of the contest became extremely worried. Already three men had been killed. Some of the nine planes gathered at the dusty Oakland airfield obviously weren't ready to fly.

Angel of Los Angeles, *an entrant in the Dole race, crashed during a test flight a few days before the takeoff, killing pilot A. V. Rogers.*

The aircraft had not been tested with their full one-ton loads of fuel. An inspector found the compass of one plane to be forty-five degrees off true direction; this would have caused the plane to miss the Hawaiian Islands, a target three hundred miles wide, and run out of gasoline somewhere in the ocean.

On August 11, the federal official in charge of the takeoff said, "In the interest of aviation and humanity this race should not be held tomorrow. It would be suicidal." The start was postponed until noon Tuesday, August 16.

The night before the rescheduled departure, the ninth plane in the starting list was ordered out of the race when the official committee decided that it couldn't carry enough fuel for the Pacific crossing. If the plane took off, the committee said, it would fall into the ocean three hundred miles short of Hawaii. Although the committee probably saved the pilot's life, the plane's owners became angry because it wasn't allowed to race. Such was the itchy eagerness of pilots and sponsors to challenge the ocean, even when common sense said the dice were loaded against them.

Fog covered the Oakland field on the morning of August 16, helping to smother the dust stirred by thousands of automobiles as spectators swarmed onto the field for the start. By midmorning 75,000 persons had gathered, fighting for vantage points along the fence that bordered the 7,000-foot runway. The crowd grew to more than 100,000—some newspapers claimed 200,000—by noon. Police battled to keep spectators off the runway. Fire engines and ambulances were stationed along the route, and a hospital tent was put up to receive casualties. Tension had grown. Tractors pulled heavy rollers along the runway to smooth the bumps, and a horse-drawn water wagon soaked it.

The feminine star of the show, Mildred Doran, arrived at the headquarters tent carrying sandwiches she had made for the crew. She expressed smiling confidence. Mildred was tiny, weighing little more than a hundred pounds, and was described by a writer as "unaffected and unpainted." She wore an outfit of khaki that looked like a uniform, with an overseas cap, a mannish shirt and necktie, and a Sam Brown belt, the decorative piece

172

*Mildred Doran wearing the special uniform she had made for her
ill-fated flight to Hawaii*

of leather harness army officers used to wear. With this military-like garb she wore golf stockings and two-toned sport shoes. Perhaps she thought she was setting a style trend. On her uniform coat she wore five fraternity pins, tokens of love from Michigan State college men. She fit a frequently heard description about girls of that day, "the cutest little thing."

Mildred talked about going into the movies and told reporters, "I'm not a bit worried about the flight, although I suppose I should be."

Poor Mildred Doran! She hadn't seen what a feminine friend in Michigan had written about her in the Honolulu *Star-Bulletin*: "She didn't know enough to be afraid."

As the Dole Derby's only passenger, she had a unique position. There wasn't much for her to do and no obvious place in the plane for her to sit. Behind the cockpit of the red-and-white biplane *Miss Doran*, carpenters had built a partition with a circular hole near the top. The partition created a compartment the width of the plane and three feet deep. This was to be Mildred's space during the long flight. It contained a wide cushioned seat, on which she could half lie down. She had a small megaphone, like those cheerleaders use. To communicate with pilot Auggy Pedlar and navigator Vilas H. Knope above the roar of the motor, she put the megaphone through the hole in the partition and shouted.

Shortly before 10:00 A.M., the eight planes that had actually made it to the starting line were wheeled into position at the head of the runway and drawn up in a semicircle. At the starter's signal they were to taxi onto the runway in sequence and take off.

Trying to relax the tension of waiting, the participants bragged how they would reach Honolulu first and what they would do when they got there. Captain William P. Erwin of the *Dallas Spirit* asserted, "When I get to Honolulu, I'm going to find the dancing party wearing the reed skirt and thank her for guiding me in, because when I pass the halfway mark I'm going to listen for the rustling of breezes and use it as a beacon."

If the participants were secretly frightened, they concealed

174

the fact very well. Martin Jensen, who resided in Hawaii, quipped, "My wife told me before I took the steamer for San Francisco that if I flopped into the ocean, she was going to row out and smack me over the head with an oar. So I guess I've got to make it."

He was able to be in the race because his wife had helped raise the $15,000 to buy his plane, which he christened the *Aloha* with a bottle of water he had brought to California from Waikiki Beach.

The sun was bright when race time came at noon. That, the generally jaunty air of the racers, and the excited mood of the crowd created a holiday air.

When the starter waved a checkered flag, Bennett Griffin opened the throttle of his *Oklahoma*. Down the runway it bumped past the reviewing stand of special guests, and into the air. Cheers from the spectators followed the plane as it headed west across San Francisco Bay toward the Golden Gate. The cheers turned to screams as *El Encanto*, the second plane piloted

Helmeted Major Livingston Irving stands in front of his Dole entry, Pabco Flyer. *The plane crashed during takeoff in the race, but Irving escaped from the wreckage.*

by Lieutenant Norman A. Goddard, cartwheeled during takeoff on its left wing into a pile of wreckage. Suddenly the race didn't seem quite so much fun. Goddard and his navigator staggered away from the wreckage, to lusty cheers.

Next to try was the *Pabco Flyer*, in which Major Livingston Irving was attempting a solo flight without a navigator. As things turned out, he didn't need one. The *Pabco Flyer* rose a few feet, settled to earth again, and finally stuck in the marsh at the end of the runway. After it was pulled free, Irving made another attempt. This time the *Pabco Flyer* rose seventy feet, dipped its nose, and smashed into the ground. Irving luckily escaped.

The carnage was growing. Two crashes out of three takeoff attempts.

The most eye-catching plane in the race, and many observers believed the best, was the streamlined *Golden Eagle*. Its golden wings and fuselage gleamed in the sun as Jack Frost put it smoothly into the air.

Next came *Miss Doran*. As she climbed aboard, Mildred was asked for her last words. "I haven't any but goodbye and I love you," she replied. "Afraid? Of course not. I'm happy and ready to go." Minutes later Auggy Pedlar got *Miss Doran* airborne. Things were looking up. Always boosting Hawaii, Martin Jensen tossed flower leis from the cockpit of *Aloha* as it gathered speed and took off. Art Goebel got his *Woolaroc* off safely. Finally, the silver fuselage and green wings of the *Dallas Spirit* with Captain William F. Erwin at the controls rose into the sky.

Not so bad, after all, the crowd agreed. Six of the eight entries were in the sky and on their way. Spectators began to leave. But then, what was this? A plane was coming back. Coughing and sputtering, the *Miss Doran* had returned only eleven minutes after it took off. Airmen in the crowd cocked their heads and listened uneasily. That plane didn't sound right for a 2,400-mile ocean flight. Pedlar fiddled with the engine, changed a sparkplug, and said, "Let's go again."

Mildren Doran watched uneasily as repairs were made, but when Pedlar suggested that she stay behind, she refused. Her face turned white but her courage didn't waver. "I'm going!"

The plane headed toward the ocean in good style.

Within minutes, two more starters returned. The *Oklahoma* had suffered a rip in her canvas fuselage, and the *Dallas Spirit* had trouble with her steering mechanism. Repairs would take a day or two.

Altogether, after the crashes and the false starts, four of the eight planes actually were on their way across the Pacific, reaching for that $25,000—only four of the original fifteen entrants. They were the *Golden Eagle, Aloha, Woolaroc,* and *Miss Doran.*

The next morning brought a shift in the action. Now the scene was Wheeler Field, the United States Army field northwest of Honolulu. Through the long night of August 16-17, the rival planes droned across the Pacific, flying about ninety miles an hour at altitudes of one to two thousand feet. The only plane whose whereabouts were fairly well known was Goebel's *Woolaroc,* which alone carried a two-way radio. That strange name, incidentally, supposedly was an Indian good luck name borrowed from an Oklahoma chief.

Lines of automobiles paraded out from the city to the field early in the morning. Soon a crowd of twenty thousand, extremely large for Hawaii, had gathered to cheer the planes as they arrived.

No doubt existed about who was their favorite—Martin Jensen, their own native son, in *Aloha.* Many enthusiasts had waited all night for good positions, although realists knew that no plane would arrive before mid-morning. Rumors circulated that this contestant, or that one, had been sighted flying in from the sea. The only confirmed information was that Goebel had exchanged radio messages with a ship not quite five hundred miles from Honolulu and was on course.

The morning passed, but no planes arrived. Expectation turned into concern. Then, a few minutes after noon, a monoplane appeared on the horizon, approaching the field from downtown Honolulu.

"Is it Jensen?" the spectators asked each other.

As the plane slipped in for a smooth landing, they saw it was the *Woolaroc.* Goebel taxied close to the grandstand, cut the

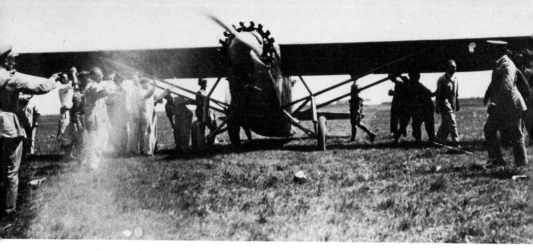

The Woolaroc, *piloted by Arthur Goebel, taxis up to the grandstand at* *Wheeler Field, Honolulu, upon arrival from San Francisco, as wel-* *comers gather to greet it.*

motor and climbed stiffly out. Girls placed leis around his neck in the traditional Hawaiian welcome and sang native melodies. The Army fired a welcoming salute. The crowd broke through the military lines around the plane.

"How many others are in ahead of me?" the pilot asked.

"Nobody. You won!"

"Honest to gosh, do you mean that I am really the first one here?" Goebel grinned and waved, jubilant at collecting $25,000.

The trip, he said, was uneventful. He and his navigator, Lieutenant W.V. Davis, had just plugged along hour after hour. Because of the shape of the *Woolaroc's* cabin, they could not see each other, so they sent messages back and forth by wires and pulleys. They hadn't used the smelling salts Goebel brought along to keep them awake. The *Woolaroc* had been airborne for 26 hours, 17 minutes, and 33 seconds, averaging ninety-two miles an hour.

Goebel told Jensen's worried wife that he hadn't seen or heard from her husband since they crossed the California coast a full day earlier. Concern turned to joy two hours later when another plane appeared above the field. This time it was the gaily painted yellow and red *Aloha,* landing after 28 hours and 16 minutes aloft. The crowd yelled with pleasure at the realization that their local hero was safe and had won $10,000.

His feet on the ground once more, Jensen explained, "We got lost, but after four hours' wandering we soon found ourselves and lit out like a blue streak for Wheeler Field." Jensen's navigator, Paul Schluter, stretched his legs in relief. He was a ship's officer, recruited to assist Jensen at the last moment. This race was the first time he had ever been in an airplane!

Although the crowd began breaking up, hundreds waited to welcome the *Golden Eagle* and *Miss Doran*. They were expected at any minute.

They waited . . . and waited. Hours passed with no word. Reluctantly, race officials admitted the truth. Both planes were missing. The optimists among them explained cheerfully, "If they were forced down at sea, the planes are buoyant and can float until someone reaches them."

By the next morning, even the optimists of the previous day were grim. The planes would long since have run out of gas. The United States Navy had dispatched forty surface vessels and submarines, including an aircraft carrier, to search the route.

Martin Jensen's Aloha, *second-place winner in the Dole Derby, is inspected by Hawaiian children.*

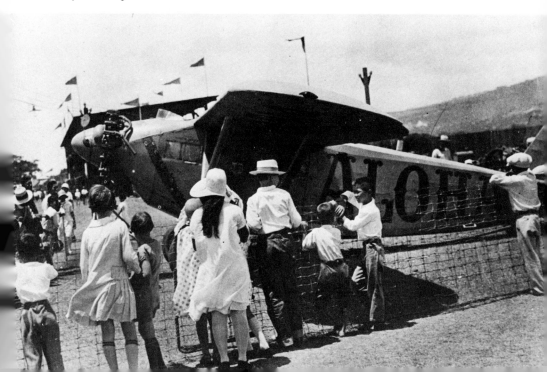

Merchant ships along the path were given radio instructions about where to hunt.

Rewards of $40,000 were posted for recovery of the missing planes. Hawaii was full of rumors that one of the planes had been found. One such report was cabled back to Michigan, somehow turning into confirmed fact en route, and was announced from the stage of a Flint theater. This touched off a parade celebrating the rescue of Mildred Doran. When a denial arrived later, the city's ministers conducted community prayers for her safety.

Five more lives had been added to the Dole Derby's death toll. The elaborate celebration for the winners was canceled, and Dole handed them their checks in a subdued ceremony.

Distressing as the story of the Dole Derby had become, a tragic final chapter still was to be written. When the *Dallas Spirit* developed trouble with its controls after takeoff, pilot Erwin and navigator A.H. Eichwaldt had returned to Oakland. They worked on repairs while the four rival planes flew toward Honolulu. By Friday morning the *Dallas Spirit* was ready to fly again. The two men announced they would make the Oakland–Honolulu flight, even though the race was over; along the way they would search the ocean for wreckage of the *Golden Eagle* and the *Miss Doran*.

Shortly before noon, Friday, three days after the mass takeoff, the *Dallas Spirit* flew out to sea. Her crewmen exchanged banter by radio with ships below them and land stations. All went smoothly this time—until the plane was 650 miles out over the ocean at twilight. Then a radio message from it was picked up by an Army station on the mainland:

"We were in a tailspin but came out of it O.K. But we sure were scared. It was a close call. Bill (presumably Erwin) thought it was all over, but we came out of it. The lights on the instrument panel went out, and it was so dark that. . ."

The radio signals faded away. Minutes later the land station picked them up again. "We are in a tailspin. . .SOS. . ."

After that, silence.

The sea had claimed another airplane. Two more participants

Strands of leis adorn the shoulders of pilot Arthur Goebel as he receives congratulations for winning the Dole Derby and the $25,000 prize. A Hawaiian woman with ukelele sings welcoming song in background.

James Dole, sponsor of the race to Hawaii, delivers $25,000 check to the winners, Lieutenant William V. Davis, navigator, and Arthur C. Goebel, pilot, of the Woolaroc (left), and $10,000 to Martin Jensen, pilot, and Paul Schluter, navigator, of the Aloha (right).

in the race for cash and glory were dead. That made the final toll of the race ten dead, three before takeoff and seven fallen into the sea. No trace of the missing planes was ever found. They simply vanished.

A month later, the liner *Maui* sailing from San Francisco with hundreds of passengers halted seven hundred miles at sea. The vessel circled slowly three times while passengers and crew tossed overboard hundreds of floral offerings from sympathizers throughout the United States. In the middle of this floating tribute was a large floral Bible sent by students of the Caro, Michigan, school in memory of their adventurous teacher, Mildred Doran. Those aboard the ship sang hymns and recited prayers; then the *Maui* gathered speed for Honolulu.

Editorial writers and politicians set up a cry that the Dole Derby had been a disaster and had proved that airplanes—at least land planes without pontoons—never were intended to fly across the Pacific. But if there were lessons to be learned from those who died, lessons also were to be drawn from those who succeeded. Forty years later, Goebel and Jensen once again flew to Honolulu, together this time as fellow passengers on a jet airliner. Goebel by then was a retired Air Force colonel and Jensen an aviation engineer and inventor. They agreed, and so did everyone who talked with them, that their epic race had probably been the single most important event in developing transpacific flying into the everyday operation that the world takes for granted.

182

— 11 —

"Wrong-Way" Corrigan

He was a little redheaded wisp of an Irishman in greasy work clothes, only five feet, five inches tall—the kind of man no one noticed in a crowd except perhaps when he flashed his pixy grin. His name was Douglas G. Corrigan.

When Charles A. Lindbergh took delivery of the *Spirit of St. Louis* from the Ryan factory in San Diego in the spring of 1927, the Ryan workers who had labored long hours of overtime to build the plane lined up in front of it for a photograph. Lindbergh stood tall in a dark business suit and felt hat in front of the propellor. Inconspicuously, off near the right end of the picture, smaller than any of the other men, was 20-year-old Corrigan.

Doug hadn't worked for Ryan very long. Earlier, he had done his apprenticeship as a mechanic by hanging around airfields, the "kid" on whom others played jokes. He recalled later that once a workman noticed a propellor was dirty and told Doug, "Go over to the shack for a bucket of propellor wash." The obliging young mechanic did so, only to be met with laughter when he couldn't find any. Propellor wash, he discovered, is the wind stirred up by propellors in motion.

At Ryan, Corrigan was proud that he was one of the workmen who bolted the wing of Lindbergh's plane onto the fuselage. That act gave him a personal share in Lindbergh's flight. Corrigan's admiration of Lindbergh was unbounded, and like mil-

Photograph of the workers at the Ryan Aircraft plant, San Diego, California, who built the Spirit of St. Louis. *Charles Lindbergh,*

lions of other young Americans he dreamed that someday he could fly the Atlantic solo the way his hero had done.

In Corrigan's case, the dream came true. He did fly the Atlantic single-handed, in a flight that made the world laugh not at him, but with him.

Life wasn't easy for young Doug Corrigan. His father had left the family and his mother ran rooming houses in Los Angeles until her early death. After finishing ninth grade, Doug quit school to earn money at small wages in a bottling plant, a lumber yard, and in home construction. He was bitten by the flying bug, too, and in 1925 paid $2.50 for his first airplane ride, in a Jenny. After that, nothing could keep him out of the air. Later that year, he scraped together $5.00 for his first flying lesson at the age of eighteen. He soloed in March, 1926. Between other jobs, he spent his hours around the dusty Los Angeles area flying fields. His luck turned good for the moment and he got the job at San Diego with Ryan.

After leaving the Ryan company, Corrigan became a job

wearing a felt hat, is standing in front of the propellor. The short
man in work clothes seventh from the right is Douglas Corrigan.

gypsy, working wherever a mechanic's position was available
and flying in his spare time when he could get the use of an airplane. He earned his transport pilot's license, although it didn't
do him much good.

At one time he worked at the new airfield at Palm Springs,
California, which was only a few acres of soft desert sand on land
owned by the Indians. He and others dragged a smooth strip
on the sand and soaked it, baking the crust hard under the intense sun. Thus they could take off and land without the wheels
sinking into the earth.

As a barnstormer, Corrigan reached the East Coast at Virginia
Beach, Virginia. He and his partner obtained use of a field eighty
feet wide and six hundred feet long, from which to carry passengers. At one end was a cornfield. In order to have enough takeoff room, the flyers paid the farmer to cut the tops off the corn.
However, the corn kept growing. Later, in his book *That's My
Story*, Corrigan remembered, "We were picking cornstalks off
the landing gear and tail surfaces after every flight." Once the

right wing caught in the cornstalks. "We pulled the plane out of the cornfield and pulled about three bushels of corn off the wings and kept on flying."

The future hero learned about flying the hard way.

Late in 1931 he was on the East Coast and wanted to return to California. Despite the Depression, he had accumulated a little money. For $325 he bought a second-hand Curtiss Robin monoplane. That battered craft was to carry him to international renown later, but only after years of penny-pinching and wandering.

Doug and his brother Harry started west in the newly acquired plane, carrying everything they owned. They used a roadmap as a guide, stopping in fields to earn a few dollars carrying passengers. They slept in the plane or on the ground. Several times they had to patch the Robin's fabric cover; once they bought gasoline from the tank of a farmer's tractor to keep going. After eighteen days they reached California, having kept the plane at a regular airport only two nights.

All this time, Doug clung to his hope of flying the Atlantic, Lindbergh style. As the Depression years of the Thirties moved along, a few more Atlantic flights were made by well-prepared expeditions, but regular passenger flights still were not practical.

Corrigan fell in love with that plane of his. He fussed over it the way young men today pamper their automobiles. Every spare dime he had went into improving it. There never was much money because he frequently was out of a job and broke. The Curtiss Robin had been built to carry four persons on rather short flights. Doug decided to remodel it as a single-seater and install extra fuel tanks where the seats had been. Being a welder, he built and installed the tanks himself. He made a deal to buy a secondhand Wright J6-5 engine and installed it in place of the Robin's original one. The engine, built in 1929 like the plane itself, developed 165 horsepower—not much by the rapidly improving standards of the mid-1930's but greater than the original.

Doing everything himself, Corrigan stripped the original fabric cover from the wing and fuselage, put on a new covering, and treated the body with preservative "dope." A friend who

186

Douglas "Wrong-Way" Corrigan in the cockpit of his plane

flew with him at that time told how they landed in a cow pasture and Corrigan insisted on sleeping with the plane that night. He knew that cows loved the taste of the fabric "dope" and feared they might eat the covering of the fuselage. He also installed new wheels.

As he kept remodeling the aging plane, Corrigan made cross-country trips in it to check his long-distance navigation. Nothing seemed to matter much to him except that plane. His friends jokingly called it the "Corrigan Clipper."

During the 1930's airplanes became larger, faster, sleeker, and more powerful. Corrigan's Robin looked more and more out-of-date, a fragile leftover from the pioneering days of the 1920's. It was smaller than Lindbergh's *Spirit of St. Louis* and carried less fuel. Federal regulations on planes and pilots grew much more stringent, too. The happy-go-lucky days of barnstorming were dying. Flying any place you wished, in any old "crate" you could coax into the air, was frowned upon. Aviation was becoming a business, not a gathering place for free souls like Douglas Corrigan.

He applied to the federal government in 1937 for a permit to fly from New York to London but was turned down. The inspectors needed only one look at "Corrigan's Clipper" to know that flying it over the Atlantic was a form of suicide they didn't intend to endorse.

Doug was out of a job again but worked through the winter of 1937 and spring of 1938 as an aircraft welder in Southern California. He was thirty-one years old. At night and on weekends, he flew his cherished plane on test flights. Grudgingly, a federal inspector granted him an experimental license for a nonstop flight from Los Angeles to New York, with the understanding that he could make the return nonstop trip westbound if everything went right.

Without fuss, and telling only a few friends he was going, Corrigan took off from Long Beach, California, on July 8, 1938, for New York with 252 gallons of gasoline. He figured he got about eleven miles to the gallon, so with luck and a tailwind he might make the trip nonstop. Experiments had shown that the plane got the best results by puttering along at eighty-five miles an hour, rather than being pushed at top speed of a little above a hundred.

The weather was rough and he needed twenty-seven hours to do it, but Corrigan landed the Robin at Roosevelt Field on Long Island after crossing the United States nonstop. Whenever he became sleepy, he stuck his head out the window and let the wind rouse him. Precisely four gallons of gasoline were left in the tanks when he landed. Although transcontinental nonstop flights still were far from common, hardly anyone noticed his feat. That suited him just fine.

One of those Corrigan did talk to during the next few days around Roosevelt Field was a prominent woman pilot, Ruth Nichols. He told her he was going to make a nonstop flight back to California via a southern route. Noticing that he didn't have a parachute, she offered to lend him one. He said no thanks because there wasn't room for one, and anyway the plane was

Douglas Corrigan stands in front of the rebuilt plane in which he flew the Atlantic from New York to Ireland.

all he had and if it fell to pieces he would go with it.

Indeed, Corrigan had practically nothing, not even a change of clothes with him. His plane had only the simplest instruments to guide it, and a map of the United States aboard showing his planned route back to the West Coast, south down the Atlantic seaboard and then westward across the southern United States to Los Angeles. During several cloudy days, Corrigan hung around the airfields and watched the weather reports. While waiting, he patched the weak spots in the plane's fabric.

On Saturday the sixteenth the weather was good all across the United States, and he told people he would leave early the next morning. He flew the Robin a short hop over to Floyd Bennett Field and taxied it to a commercial hangar. There he gave the engine a grease job and had the gasoline tanks filled, 320 gallons, paying $62.26 in cash for the fuel.

Corrigan wanted to take off just after midnight because, he said, he hoped to have moonlight that night for his flight over the American desert. Looking at the badly overloaded, battered plane, the airport manager refused permission for departure until dawn. He ordered flares ignited along the runway as an additional safety factor and had a fire engine standing by.

At dawn Sunday, Corrigan turned over the propellor himself, checked the engine for loose parts, and climbed into the plane. Because the knob was broken, he tied the door shut with bailing wire. For food, he had a box of fig cookies and candy bars. With a wave to the handful of persons around the hangar, he made a long, laborious takeoff, rising barely fifty feet off the ground at the edge of the field. "Corrigan's Clipper" groaned under the load; it had never before carried such weight and wasn't built for it.

Doug had taken off toward the east. The spectators watched for him to bank and head south and west for California. But he didn't. Instead, the plane was seen angling to the northeast.

"That's all right. He'll make the turn after he has gone a few miles and gained some altitude," one of the watchers said.

Corrigan's version of what happened after that sounds like an Irish fairy tale. In fact, it was just that, an elfin yarn spun with a straight face. It went like this:

As he gained altitude and prepared to turn west, he saw that one of the two compasses in the cabin was not working because the liquid had leaked out, a mishap he hadn't noticed earlier when he checked the plane in the dark. However, since the second compass on the floor had been set to fly a westerly course, he turned the plane until the parallel lines matched. By then, he was into fog; he climbed above it and flew on, following the compass needle.

About two hours later, he saw a city through a gap in the fog which he assumed was Baltimore, Maryland. Later he figured out that it must have been Boston, Massachusetts.

Still flying above the fog ten hours later, along what he as-sumed was a westward course, he felt his feet getting cold. No wonder they were chilly: they were soaked with gasoline leak-ing from the main tank. This didn't worry him much, because he assumed he could always land if the leak grew worse. During the night, the leakage did increase. Pointing his flashlight down, he saw gasoline an inch deep on the cabin floor. He punched a hole in the floor with a screwdriver and let the gasoline drain out into the air below, carefully picking a spot for the hole so the inflammable dripping wouldn't hit the red-hot exhaust pipe.

Corrigan had planned to fly slowly to save gasoline, but the leak caused him to speed up, on the theory that the faster he flew, the sooner he would reach California and the less time there would be for gasoline to drip out.

The American newspapers were puzzled in their Monday morning editions. Corrigan's plane had not been seen since it took off nearly twenty-four hours earlier. What had become of him? They published headlines like "Mystery Flight" and "Vanishes Eastward."

After flying all night, Corrigan came down through the clouds and was, he claimed, puzzled to see water below him instead of land. Since he had been flying "only" twenty-six hours without a stop, he figured that he shouldn't be over the Pacific Ocean yet. At this point, so he said, he discovered what he had done wrong. He realized that he had been following the wrong end of the magnetic compass needle the entire flight, and it had pointed him over the Atlantic Ocean instead of toward California!

He had just eaten some fig cookies when he noticed land below the plane. Crossing the green coastal hills, where there were no towns, he flew inland for about forty-five minutes until he reached ocean again. This, he decided, must be Ireland. And it was!

Flying south, Corrigan found a large airport with the name Baldonnell marked on it. He knew this was Dublin so he landed, after being in the air for twenty-eight hours and thirteen minutes.

An army officer walked up to the plane, and Corrigan said to him, "My name's Corrigan. I got mixed up in the clouds and must have flown the wrong way."

That was his story.

When word flashed back to the United States about his remarkable flight, he immediately became known as "Wrong-Way" Corrigan. Nobody believed his tale, and aviation experts were astounded that he had crossed the ocean in such a "crate," but the world cheered his audacity and flying skill. He was a hero who didn't look or act like one, a blithe individualist who had thumbed his nose at the authorities and at the laws of prob-

191

ability and gotten away with it. Not only had he flown the Atlantic without an American permit, but he had lacked permission to land at Dublin. For once, however, government officials had a sense of humor.

As Corrigan boarded an ocean liner at Cobh, Ireland, for the trip home, he was handed a cablegram from the United States Department of Commerce announcing his punishment for breaking the law. His pilot's license was suspended until August 4. That was the day the ship was due in New York. In other words, no punishment at all.

Back in the United States, Doug received the celebrity treatment—a ticker-tape parade in New York City, a meeting with President Franklin D. Roosevelt at the White House, and a nationwide tour in the faithful old Robin. Wherever he went, his hosts gave him joke gifts. The Liars Club of Burlington, Wisconsin, elected him a member. Many cities presented him with compasses. At Tulsa, Oklahoma, an Indian tribe initiated him as Chief Wrong-Way, and Abilene, Texas, gave him a watch that ran backward.

Douglas Corrigan was the poor man's hero, shy and modest.

Never once in public did he budge from his story that, "Man, I didn't mean to do this at all."

In later years, Corrigan settled on a twenty-acre citrus ranch in Southern California and enjoyed a comfortable life. He kept the sturdy but shabby plane in a shed at his home, as a reminder of his moment of glory. It was a reminder, too, of an era gone, because Corrigan's adventure was the last of the transatlantic daredevil flights. Aviation had turned into big business.

— 12 —

Amelia Vanishes

For nine years after her adventure as the first woman to fly the Atlantic, aboard the *Friendship*, Amelia Earhart was the most famous American heroine. Slim and cool, boyish in appearance with her short cropped hair, this business-like young woman often referred to herself as AE. She added one aerial record after another to demonstrate that a woman was capable of achieving as much as a man. Aviation was a splendid field for this purpose. It belonged almost exclusively to men in the early days. When a feminine flyer showed that she could do as well as men had done, her success drew widespread attention. Nobody talked about "women's liberation" in the late 1920's and 1930's, but Amelia was an example of what it meant.

While the *Friendship* flight had made her known everywhere, she was actually embarrassed about it. She felt that she was receiving credit she didn't deserve, because she hadn't flown the plane or done its navigating. She had been a glorified passenger, which wasn't her way of doing things. That, she said, was flying under false colors.

Three years after the *Friendship* flight, in 1931, Amelia Earhart married George Palmer Putnam, a prominent book publisher and later a motion picture executive. He not only took a background role to his wife but worked diligently to arrange and promote the series of long-distance, speed, and high-altitude

194

The resemblance between Amelia Earhart and Charles A. Lindbergh is especially evident in this picture of her taken beside the plane in which she sought to fly around the world.

flights she made. When people half jokingly called him "Mr. Earhart," he didn't mind.

At breakfast a few months after their marriage, while they were eating and reading the morning newspaper, Amelia said almost casually, "Would you mind if I flew the Atlantic?"

It was hardly the kind of question a wife tossed at her husband in those days. Putnam thought it was a splendid idea, however. This time, Amelia was going to make the flight alone, doing the flying and navigating.

She purchased a used but good Lockheed Vega monoplane and had a new engine installed. Her plans were kept quiet. With two expert men flyers along for advice, she flew the plane to Harbor Grace, Newfoundland, the jumping-off place for her oceanic attempt. Her husband stayed behind in New York.

Amelia Earhart took off alone across the Atlantic on May 20, 1932, exactly five years after Charles A. Lindbergh made his Paris flight. The Atlantic sky was up to its old tricks—clouds, fog, and the perilous coating of ice accumulating on the wings of AE's Vega. But she pushed ahead through the night and the next afternoon landed her plane in a pasture near Londonderry, Ireland, scattering grazing cows with the roar of her engine.

A woman had flown the Atlantic for the first time, solo. Amelia felt vindicated. Nobody could call her a "phony" heroine now,

Three famous flyers of the 1930's—Amelia Earhart, Wiley Post, and Roscoe Turner

not even herself. During the next five years she achieved speed and distance records and served as an effective promoter of aviation through lectures and writing.

Then early in 1937, she announced plans for the longest and most difficult trip of all, a flight around the world staying as close to the equator as possible. This would be a distance of 27,000 miles. Just a few years earlier, a woman pilot who attempted such a journey over long stretches of water and poorly marked regions of Africa and Asia would have been greeted with universal skepticism. When Amelia Earhart was the one involved, public reaction was, "It will be dangerous, but she can do it." That was precisely what she believed. She planned to pay part of the trip's cost by carrying letter covers that would be sold to stamp collectors.

First, she needed a plane. It had to be dependable and capable of carrying large gasoline supplies for the long hops involved. The plane she chose was built especially for her by the Lockheed Aircraft Corporation in Southern California—a monoplane with two engines called an Electra. With its passenger seats replaced by extra fuel tanks, it had an extreme range of four thousand miles, very far for the 1930's. Dressed in a mechanic's overalls, Amelia worked with the Lockheed builders as they installed the navigation equipment.

Although the Electra was considered very modern, it had one aspect that seems strange today, considering that by 1937 aviation had advanced so far in design. Amelia and the navigator who would accompany her, Fred Noonan, could not talk directly with each other. If the navigator needed to give the pilot a message, he either stretched it forward to her clipped to the end of a cut-down bamboo fishing pole, or he had to crawl along a catwalk over the extra gasoline tanks installed behind the pilot's seat.

Originally, they were to fly around the world east-to-west from California to Honolulu and then on across the Pacific. When Amelia took off from Hawaii, however, something went wrong. A wing scraped the ground, and the plane was damaged seriously. It had to be brought back to the mainland for repairs.

Amelia Earhart rests against a wall for a few moments while supervising construction of the plane that carried her to a mysterious death in 1937.

At that point, Amelia decided to reverse her plans and circle the globe in the opposite direction, west to east.

In flying around the world close to the equator, AE knew that the greatest peril lay in crossing the Pacific Ocean. The Army aviators in 1924 in their World Cruisers used a far North Pacific route so they could make short hops along the Aleutian Island chain. She must cross seven thousand miles of water with only two stopping places, tiny Howland Island and the Hawaiian Islands.

A quick study of the globe showed that the key to her flight, indeed her survival, would be her ability to fly 2,500 miles over water northeast from New Guinea and land at Howland Island, a speck of land in the South Pacific. It was a tiny target, indeed, a half-mile wide and two miles long, a treeless sandspit rising a few feet above the water and surrounded by hundreds of miles of ocean. This was a formidable challenge for an airplane whose radio equipment had a relatively short range; use of radar still was several years in the future. Amelia was confident, however.

She and Fred Noonan began their round-the-world flight in the Electra from Oakland, California, and then took off from Miami, Florida, on June 1, 1937, heading southeast to Puerto Rico. All went well. Over ocean, jungle, and desert the Electra flew to South America, then across the South Atlantic to Dakar on the western bulge of Africa. From Dakar, Amelia and Noonan flew an almost uncharted route eastward for 4,300 miles—in the 1930's airplanes rarely used this remote aerial path.

Noonan wrote home to his wife, "Our flights over the desert were more difficult than over water. That was because the maps of the country are very inaccurate and consequently extremely misleading. In fact, at points no dependence at all could be placed on them. Also recognizable landmarks are few and far between . . . there were times when I wouldn't have bet a nickel on the accuracy of our assumed position."

Across Africa they went, and then Asia. Their route took them to exotic-sounding places. Newspaper readers in the United States had a geography lesson as they followed the daily bulletins of their progress: Khartoum, Massaua, Eritrea; across the Red Sea to Karachi, India; over the Ganges River to Calcutta; Rangoon, Burma; Singapore, a stop in Java, and on to Port Darwin, Australia. A month away from home, on June 30, 1937, Amelia landed the plane at Lae, New Guinea. The globe-girdlers had

Seated in the unfinished cabin of her Lockheed Electra, Amelia Earhart examines blueprints of her around-the-world plane.

flown more than twenty thousand miles across some of the most remote places on earth and had reached the critical moment, that stretch of seven thousand miles of Pacific Ocean back to the West Coast of the United States.

Fatigue was overpowering them. Day after day, they rose before dawn for early takeoffs, then arrived at airports that often were difficult to find and not much to see when they got there. Once they were past Howland Island, sitting far out in the Pacific vastness, they would be on the home stretch—first the Hawaiian Islands and then the final lap to the mainland on a course Amelia knew well.

The plane's radio had a range of approximately five hundred miles. Thus the flyers would have radio contact back to Lae for a few hours. After that they would fly through the night across the Pacific without radio contact, until they could be picked up by radios on the United States Coast Guard cutter *Itasca*, stationed at Howland for that purpose. Theoretically, the plane then would be about five hundred miles out from Howland and could ride in to the island on the radio beam transmitted by the *Itasca*. That left a gap of about fifteen hundred miles during which Amelia and Noonan would be without the ability to check their position by radio. Their route through the darkness would be determined by celestial navigation, by Noonan's "shooting" the stars to determine their position.

It was perilous business. If they miscalculated, they would miss Howland and the even smaller Baker Island to the south and almost inevitably splash down in the Pacific after running out of gas. The plane might float for a few hours while rescuers sought them. But it would be such a tiny object in such a huge ocean . . .

The flyers took off from Lae at 10:00 A.M. on July 2 northeast across the ocean into a mystery that never has been solved.

Heavy headwinds slowed their progress. In late afternoon, Amelia radioed their position—right on course—back to Lae, then passed out of that airfield's radio range.

At two forty-five the next morning, the *Itasca* at Howland heard its first words from the plane. Hardly distinguishable be-

A smiling Amelia Earhart stands in the cockpit of her around-the-world plane, built especially for her in Southern California by the Lockheed Aircraft Corporation. She is studying the blueprints.

cause of static, Amelia was heard to say, "Cloudy and overcast . . ." What would those conditions do to Noonan's navigation by the stars?

During the next hours, the *Itasca* transmitted to the plane frequently on two wave lengths but in return heard only brief, garbled sounds. Then at 6:45 A.M., Amelia's voice came in clearly. "Please take a bearing on us and report in half an hour. I will make noise in microphone. About one hundred miles out." The message was so short that the radiomen at Howland could not determine a bearing from it.

Nearly an hour passed in which the *Itasca* received no answers to its messages. At 7:42 A.M., Amelia's voice came in again, with tension and excitement. "We must be on you. But cannot see you. But gas is running low. Been unable to reach you by radio. We are flying at altitude 1,000 feet."

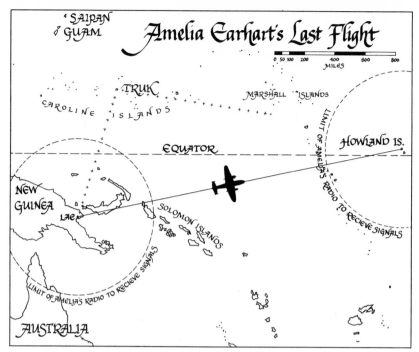

Solid line shows Amelia Earhart's flight plan; broken crosses show the theoretical secret mission over Truk to landing in the Marshalls.

Urgently, the *Itasca* signaled to the plane, asking it to respond on one of the two wave lengths assigned to it, but without response. The plane's call letters were KHAQQ.

At 8:33 A.M. the *Itasca* called to KHAQQ, "Will you please come in and answer on 3,105. We are transmitting constantly on 7,500 kilocycles. We do not hear you on 3,105..."

No answer from Amelia. Twelve minutes later, her voice came in again, clear but excited. "We are in a line of position 157-337.... We are running north and south."

Those were the last words ever heard from Amelia Earhart.

Nobody on the ship knew quite what they meant. While she obviously intended them as an indication of position, they were too vague. For days, Navy ships and airplanes searched 136,000 square miles of the Pacific, hoping to find the plane afloat. No trace was discovered. The heroine of aviation—so self-confident, so skilled, and so determined—and her navigator had missed their island target and disappeared. When the news reached the United States, many persons found it hard to believe. They hoped for a long time that the flyers would be found alive, that perhaps they had landed safely on a remote island and awaited rescue.

That isn't the end of the story, however. In those years of the late 1930's, the warlords of the Japanese imperial government were secretly fortifying some South Pacific islands, a strategy that the world learned later was a preliminary move to their treacherous attack on the United States Navy at Pearl Harbor in Hawaii on December 7, 1941, which plunged the United States into World War II.

This fact led to rumors that Amelia and Noonan hadn't been lost at sea but had been captured by the Japanese. Many Americans wanted to believe the unverified reports, since if true they would mean that the flyers were alive somewhere.

After the war ended in 1945, a fresh incident stirred up the captivity story anew. A woman native of Saipan, an island hundreds of miles north and west of Howland held by the Japanese before and during the war, told American officers that in 1937 as a young girl at Tanapag Harbor on that island she had seen a two-motored silver plane land. A little later, she saw a slender American woman with short hair, dressed in shirt and pants, and

Amelia Earhart in front of the Lockheed Electra plane in which she vanished while flying around the world in 1937. The plane was later reported seen off course in the Japanese mandated islands.

a tall man, also apparently American. They had been taken into custody as spies and were shot, she had heard. After looking at photographs, she was certain they were Amelia and Noonan.

If they were, how did they get so far off course that their plane would arrive at Saipan? A search for clues in Japanese military records, made available to American inspection after Japan's surrender, gave no answer.

One man who became intrigued with the Earhart disappearance was a San Francisco radio announcer, Fred Goerner. He spent many months investigating it during the 1960's, including four trips to the Pacific Islands. After weighing the bits of evidence and suppositions, some of them conflicting, he published a book, *The Search for Amelia Earhart*, in which he offered his theory of what happened.

When Amelia and Noonan left Lae, he reasoned, they did not fly directly toward Howland Island as announced but made a detour north to Truk, an island fortified by the Japanese in the Central Carolines. Their purpose was to observe the secret Japanese airfields and fleet facilities on Truk, for the benefit of American military intelligence. Their plane, he believed, had the range and speed to make the detour to Truk and still reach Howland safely. After flying over Truk, he asserted, they headed for Howland but ran into tropical storms and became lost. Amelia believed she had overshot Howland, turned in the wrong direction over the ocean, and finally landed safely on a tiny Japanese-controlled island in the southeastern Marshall Islands. There they were taken prisoner and eventually taken to Japanese headquarters in Saipan, to die from mistreatment or execution.

Perhaps Goerner's theory is the way it actually happened. Or perhaps Amelia simply missed Howland Island in heavy clouds and crashed into the sea. We may never know.

Her disappearance along with Fred Noonan not only cost the lives of a daring pair of flyers but brought an end to the pioneer era of aviation. Except for the surprise flight by "Wrong-Way" Corrigan the following year, Amelia's fatal journey was the last personal exploit of flying's youthful decades. Indeed, one reason Corrigan was refused official permission for his transatlantic trip was the government's clampdown on individual distance flights that followed the loss of Amelia.

By 1937, large flying boats were making survey flights across the Atlantic in preparation for the start of transatlantic passenger service. Two years after AE and Noonan disappeared, World War II began with the German invasion of Poland. Suddenly, airplanes were not regarded as flying machines intended for fun and adventure but as dealers of death by bombs and bullets, operating in gigantic formations. Thousands of warplanes were flown from the United States to European battlefields, and across the Pacific. Instead of reading about the daredevil actions of individual pilots, the public was absorbed with stories of mass bombing raids by waves of planes sent out according to grand strategic plans. Often these raids were directed by one-time barnstormers who had won high rank in the Army Air Corps. Almost incredible tales of heroism by pilots and crew members were reported, but these were incidental to the large-scale operations.

Under the pressure of war, spectacular improvements were made in radio communications and flight instruments. Radar was developed, so that pilots could "see" other airborne objects and ground stations could follow the movement of planes by use of ultrahigh frequency radio waves that reflected off objects and were recorded on screens.

Just after World War II came a revolutionary development that changed aviation completely. This was the creation of the jet engine.

From the days of man's first powered flight, airplanes were moved through the sky by the revolving of propellors. These whirling blades turned by engines either pushed the planes forward, as in the earliest Wright and Curtiss models, or pulled them ahead, as became common when the engine was moved to the front of the plane. Jet engines eliminated propellors and tremendously increased the speed of airplanes. A jet engine in an airplane has one or more exhaust nozzles for discharging toward the rear a jet of heated air and exhaust gases; these jets produce forward propulsion.

This Flying Fortress bomber, the Carol Jean, *shown at a U.S. Air Force base in England, was one of hundreds that raided Europe during World War II. Each bomb marking on the nose indicated participation in a raid. The eight swastikas showed how many German planes the Fortress had shot down.*

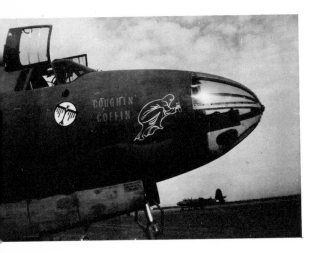

The crew of this American bomber named it the Coughin' Coffin. Markings on the other side of the nose indicated that it flew approximately fifty bombing missions from North Africa.

A load of bombs being hauled to a waiting American medium bomber at an airfield in North Africa

Jet engines were installed in military planes and then in passenger airliners. Today propellor engines are used mostly in small private recreation planes; the sight of an occasional old propellor-driven airliner makes us look up in surprise.

Jet airliners became faster and bigger during the 1960's and 1970's, until finally the swiftest commercial plane of all took to the skies. That is the Concorde. It flies faster than the speed of sound, a long hawk-beaked airliner built by the British and French which can hurtle across the Atlantic from New York to Paris in three hours and thirty minutes—one tenth the time

A formation of Flying Fortresses drops bombs on Germany during World War II. Small black clouds are bursts of flak from antiaircraft guns on the ground.

Lindbergh required to make his historic flight.

On New Year's Eve a dozen men and women in Paris toasted the arrival of the year 1977. They had just eaten the first course

The British-French Concorde carries passengers across the Atlantic Ocean faster than the speed of sound.

of an international dinner in a Parisian hotel. After the midnight hour passed, they boarded a waiting Concorde and flew west across the Atlantic faster than sound, and faster than the clock. Over the Atlantic they had the second course of dinner; when midnight came again they welcomed it while flying several miles above the ocean. The Concorde landed at Washington before 10:00 P.M. local time, and the party was whisked to the French Embassy for dessert. There, when midnight caught up with them again, they welcomed 1977 for the third time, with champagne.

Had someone able to foresee the future told Orville Wright or Lincoln Beachey or Charles Lindbergh or Art Goebel or Amelia Earhart that one day passengers would make such a fantastic flight, they would have laughed him out of the hangar. Even the pioneer men and women whose adventures made the Concorde flight possible didn't comprehend the enormous power of aviation they were unleashing and how it would change the world.

Acknowledgments and Bibliography

In writing this book and collecting the illustrations for it, I was assisted generously by numerous individuals. In particular, I express appreciation to James W. Jacobs, executive administrator of Aviation Hall of Fame, Inc.; Eleanor Wagner of the American Hall of Aviation History; R.J. Hill of Mentone, Indiana, for use of the Lawrence D. Bell photographic collection; George Chaplin, editor of the Honolulu *Advertiser*, Lyle Nelson of the Honolulu *Star-Bulletin*; Brewster C. Reynolds of the San Diego Aero-Space Museum; David Larzelere of the Flint, Michigan, *Journal*; Sue Jones of the Santa Ana, California, *Register*; and Julius Ivancsics of the South Bend *Tribune*.

Among the published sources I found most valuable were:

The Spirit of St. Louis, by Charles A. Lindbergh (Charles Scribner's Sons, 1953)

20 Hrs. 40 Mins., by Amelia Earhart (G.P. Putnam's Sons, 1928)

Daughter of the Sky, by Paul L. Briand, Jr. (Duell, Sloan and Pearce, 1960)

The Search for Amelia Earhart, by Fred Goerner (Doubleday, 1966)

The First to Fly, by Sherwood Harris (Simon & Schuster, 1970)

Los Angeles Aeronautics, 1920-1929, by D.D. Hatfield (Northrup University Press, 1973)

The Early Eagles, by Frank Donovan (Dodd, Mead, 1962)

Barnstorming, by Martin Caidin (Duell, Sloan and Pearce, 1965)

The Air Devils, by Don Dwiggins (Lippincott, 1966)

Higher, Faster and Farther, by Mark P. Friedlander, Jr., and Gene Gurney (William Morrow and Co., 1973)

The Only Way to Fly, by Robert J. Serling (Doubleday, 1976)

The United States Air Force, A Turbulent History, by Herbert Molloy Mason, Jr. (Mason/Charter, 1976)

What About the Airship? by Commander C.E. Rosendahl (Charles Scribner's Sons, 1938)

Lighter-Than-Air Flight, edited by Lt. Col. C.V. Glines, USAF (Franklin Watts, Inc., 1965)

The Motor Balloon "America," by Edward Mabley (Stephen Greene Press, 1969)

Atlantic Fever, by Edward Jablonski (Macmillan, 1972)

That's My Story, by Douglas Corrigan (E.P. Dutton, 1938)

Index

Orteig, Raymond, $25,000 prize, 125, 130, 134

Pan American Clippers, 166
Paris, 125–126, 151–152
Pedlar, Auggy, 174, 176
Pégoud, Adolphe, 42
Putnam, George Palmer, 194

Rickenbacker, Eddie, 41
Rodgers, Cal, 47–51
Roland, Ruth, 67
Roosevelt, President Franklin D., 76–77, 102, 192
Roosevelt, President Theodore, 36
Roosevelt Field, New York, 131–132, 139, 145, 153, 155, 188
Ryan Airlines, Inc., 141, 183

San Diego, California, 138, 141, 147, 150
Schluter, Paul, 179
Seattle, Washington, 77, 78–79, 85, 86
Sellers, Leigh, 69
Shenandoah, 103–105, 114–117
Silent movie flying stunts, 66–68, 71–72
Smith, Lieutenant Lowell H., 83, 85
Spirit of St. Louis, 143, 144, 145, 148–151, 153, 187
Stultz, Wilmer, 14–21

Taylor, Charles, 29, 31–32
Transatlantic passenger service begins, 166
Trans World Airlines, 98

United Airlines, 98
United States Army Air Corps, 102, 205
United States Army Air Service, 74
around-the-world flight, 77–86
United States Navy, 76, 78, 113, 115, 117, 120, 127, 136–137, 171, 179, 201, 202

Verne, Jules, 74, 77, 86

Wade, Lieutenant Leigh, 78
Washington, D.C., 89
Wellman, Walter, and airship America, 113–114
Western Airlines, 98
Wiley, Captain Herbert, 120
Wilson, President Woodrow, 89, 90
Wooster, Lieutenant Stanton H., 133, 135
Wright, Orville and Wilbur, 24, 29–35, 208

Zeppelin, Count Ferdinand von, 109
Zeppelin raids on London, 111

About the Author

PHIL AULT is a veteran newspaper editor in the United States and abroad. During World War II he was a war correspondent in North Africa and Iceland, and chief of the London bureau of United Press.

A graduate of De Pauw University, he began his career as a weekly newspaper reporter in Illinois. He worked as a correspondent and editor in Chicago and New York; later he was a newspaper executive in California, where he lived for twenty years. At present he is associate editor of the South Bend *Tribune*. He has written extensively about the West.